BEYOND OVERTHINKING

A Practical Guide to Habit Change and Self-Control for Reaching Your Goals

BRIANNA BROOKS

TABLE OF CONTENTS

THE OVERTHINKING TRAP

"The mind that is anxious about the future is miserable." – Seneca

Have you ever found yourself lying awake at night, endlessly replaying a conversation or worrying about a future event? Do you often get caught in a loop of **"what ifs"** and **"should haves"**? If so, you're not alone.

Meet Jenny. Jenny was the picture of success. A rising executive in a tech firm, she was admired for her sharp intellect, unwavering work ethic, and the quiet confidence she exuded in meetings. Colleagues often sought her advice, her sharp insights cutting through the clutter of corporate jargon. Yet, behind that composed facade, a storm raged in Jenny's mind – a relentless tempest of thoughts that never seemed to rest.

To the outside world, Jenny's life seemed flawless. But behind closed doors, her apartment often echoed with the soft tapping of her fingers against the kitchen counter, a nervous rhythm accompanying her racing thoughts. It was as if her mind was a crowded marketplace; each thought vying for attention, refusing to be silenced.

"What if I didn't word that email correctly? Will my boss think I'm incompetent?" she fretted after sending a routine message. Even simple tasks, like making dinner, became an ordeal as she second-guessed every ingredient every cooking time.

Jenny's overthinking wasn't limited to work. It seeped into every aspect of her life. A casual conversation with a friend could trigger a cascade of anxieties. "Did she mean that comment as a criticism? Am I being too sensitive?" she would wonder, analyzing every word, every inflection.

The most frustrating part was that Jenny knew her thoughts were often irrational. She knew she was capable and well-respected. But that didn't stop the relentless what-ifs and worst-case scenarios from playing on a loop in her mind.

The toll this took on Jenny was immense. Sleep became a distant memory, replaced by nights spent tossing and turning, her mind ablaze with worry. Exhaustion etched itself onto her face, dark circles under her eyes a testament to her mental turmoil. Her once vibrant social life dwindled as she canceled plans, preferring the solitude of her apartment to the risk of social faux pas that her mind inevitably magnified.

Even the simple pleasures of life, like reading a book or enjoying a meal, became tainted by her overthinking. The words on the page blurred as her mind wandered, conjuring up unrelated worries. The taste of food turned to ash in her mouth as she dissected every bite, and her appetite diminished by a knot of anxiety in her stomach.

Jenny's relationship with her boyfriend, Mark, was also strained. He tried to be supportive, but his reassurances were often brushed aside. "It's not that simple," she would retort, her voice laced with frustration. Mark could see the woman he loved disappearing into the depths of her overthinking, breaking his heart.

Jenny tried to hide her struggles, but it was becoming increasingly difficult. Her colleagues noticed her growing irritability and lack of focus. Her friends worried about her withdrawal from social events. Mark grew weary of the constant reassurance and the emotional distance that had grown between them.

Despite her intelligence, accomplishments, and outward success, she felt trapped in a prison of her own making. The overthinking, once a tool for problem-solving, had become a tyrannical force, robbing her of peace, joy, and the ability to be present in the moment. She knew she needed to find a way out of this labyrinth of worry, but the path seemed obscured by the very thoughts she sought to escape.

One evening, as she sat alone in her darkened apartment, the weight of her overthinking pressing down on her like a physical force, Jenny made a decision. She couldn't continue like this. She needed to find a way to silence the cacophony in her mind and reclaim her life. It was time to seek help, to learn how to navigate the turbulent waters of her overactive mind and find a way back to shore.

The High Cost of Overthinking

Overthinking is like a broken record stuck on repeat, replaying the same worries and doubts over and over again. It's a relentless mental churn that can leave us exhausted, anxious, and overwhelmed. While thinking things through is normal, overthinking goes beyond healthy problem-solving. It becomes a habit, a default mode of thinking that traps us in a cycle of negativity.

The Toll on Your Mental Health

Overthinking is a major contributor to mental health problems. Research has shown that it significantly increases the risk of anxiety and depression. When we overthink, we tend to focus on the negative, catastrophize situations, and create worst-case scenarios in our minds. This constant worry and rumination can lead to a downward spiral of anxiety and despair.

One study found that people who engage in rumination, a type of overthinking that involves dwelling on negative thoughts and emotions, are more likely to develop depression. Another study showed that overthinking can worsen anxiety symptoms, making it difficult to manage daily life.

The Body Keeps Score

It's not just our mental health that suffers. Overthinking takes a toll on our physical health as well. Chronic stress, often fueled by overthinking, has been linked to a wide range of health problems, including:

- **Heart Disease:** Studies have shown that people who experience high levels of stress are more likely to develop heart disease.

- **High Blood Pressure:** Chronic stress can raise blood pressure, increasing the risk of stroke and heart attack.

- **Weakened Immune System:** Stress can suppress the immune system, making us more susceptible to infections and illnesses.

- **Digestive Problems:** Stress can disrupt the digestive system, leading to symptoms like stomach pain, bloating, and constipation.

- **Sleep Disturbances:** Overthinking often leads to insomnia, further exacerbating stress and negatively impacting overall health.

When Relationships Suffer

Overthinking doesn't just affect us individually; it can also strain our relationships. When we're constantly caught up in our thoughts, being fully present with others is difficult. We may become irritable, withdrawn, or overly critical. Overthinking can also lead to communication breakdowns, as we may misinterpret others' words or actions or become overly defensive.

Productivity Takes a Nosedive

In the workplace, overthinking can be a major obstacle to productivity. When we're constantly second-guessing ourselves, making decisions and taking action is hard. We may become paralyzed by fear of making a mistake or spend so much time analyzing every detail that we never get anything done. This can lead to missed deadlines, poor performance, and frustration for both ourselves and our colleagues.

Real-Life Examples: Overthinking in Action

Let's look at some real-life examples of how overthinking can manifest:

- **The Job Interview:** You have a job interview coming up, and you start overthinking every possible question and answer. You worry about what to wear, what to say, and how you'll come across. By the time the interview arrives, you're so stressed out that you can barely think straight.

- **The Social Gathering:** You're invited to a party, but you start overthinking what to wear, what to talk about, and who you'll meet. You worry about saying something embarrassing or not fitting in. As a result, you either avoid the party altogether or spend the entire time feeling anxious and self-conscious.

- **The Relationship Doubt:** You're in a happy relationship, but you start overthinking your partner's words and actions. You wonder if they're truly happy, if they're still attracted to you, or if they're thinking about someone else. This constant doubt and insecurity can create tension in the relationship, ultimately leading to its demise.

The good news is that overthinking is a habit that can be broken. By learning to identify your triggers, challenge your negative thoughts, and practice mindfulness, you can regain control of your mind and live a more peaceful, fulfilling life.

The Urgency of Addressing Overthinking

Overthinking is not just a minor annoyance; it's a serious problem that can have devastating consequences for our mental, physical, and emotional well-being. By addressing overthinking, we can improve our health, strengthen our relationships, boost our productivity, and ultimately, live happier, more fulfilling lives.

The time to take action is now. Don't let overthinking control your life any longer. Start taking steps today to break free from this destructive habit and reclaim your peace of mind.

CHAPTER 1: UNDERSTANDING THE OVERTHINKING MIND

"The mind is a superb instrument if used rightly. Used wrongly, however, it becomes very destructive." – Eckhart Tolle.

Overthinking, a term often thrown around casually, is more than just pondering a problem. It's a relentless mental loop, a labyrinth of repetitive thoughts, worries, and analyses that can trap us in a cycle of anxiety, self-doubt, and emotional turmoil. This chapter aims to unravel this complex phenomenon, exploring its roots, characteristics, and impact on our well-being. Understanding the overthinking mind is the crucial first step toward reclaiming control and finding inner peace.

What Exactly is Overthinking?

Overthinking is a cognitive pattern characterized by excessive and intrusive thoughts that often revolve around negative emotions, past events, or potential future scenarios. It's a state of mind where we analyze, re-analyze, and over-analyze situations, decisions, and actions. Unlike productive thinking involving focused problem-solving, overthinking is unproductive and often increases stress and anxiety.

Let's delve into some of the defining characteristics of overthinking:

1. **Rumination:** The constant replaying of past events or conversations in our minds, often accompanied by feelings of regret, guilt, or shame.

2. **Worry:** Excessive concern about future events, often focusing on negative outcomes.

3. **Analysis Paralysis:** The inability to make decisions due to overanalyzing every possible option and outcome.

4. **Perfectionism:** The relentless pursuit of flawlessness, often leading to self-criticism and anxiety.

5. **Self-Doubt:** A persistent feeling of inadequacy or insecurity fueled by negative self-talk and comparisons to others.

These characteristics create a mental landscape dominated by negativity and uncertainty. The overthinking mind becomes consumed by "what ifs," regrets, and fears, making it difficult to enjoy the present moment and make confident decisions.

The Origins of Overthinking

Overthinking isn't simply a habit; it often has deeper roots. Understanding these roots is essential for developing effective strategies to overcome them. Here are some of the common factors that contribute to the development of overthinking patterns:

1. **Genetics and Personality:** Research suggests that some individuals may have a genetic predisposition to overthinking, particularly those who are naturally prone to anxiety or worry. Certain personality traits, such as perfectionism and neuroticism, can also increase the likelihood of overthinking.

2. **Past Experiences:** Traumatic events, childhood experiences, or a history of anxiety or depression can create a vulnerability to overthinking. These experiences can shape our beliefs about ourselves and the world, making us more prone to worry and negative thought patterns.

3. **Stressful Environments:** Living or working in a high-stress environment can trigger overthinking as a coping mechanism. The constant pressure and demands can lead to heightened alertness and a tendency to overanalyze situations.

4. **Cultural and Societal Factors:** Our culture often values productivity, achievement, and constant self-improvement. This emphasis on "doing more" can lead to a fear of failure and a tendency to overthink decisions in an effort to avoid mistakes.

Overthinking vs. Healthy Thinking

It's important to distinguish between overthinking and healthy thinking, as they serve different purposes and have vastly different outcomes.

Healthy Thinking:

- **Focused and Goal-Oriented:** Healthy thinking is directed toward finding solutions, making decisions, and achieving goals.

- **Constructive and Positive:** It involves generating creative ideas, exploring possibilities, and focusing on strengths.

- **Based on Facts and Logic:** It relies on evidence and rational analysis to reach conclusions.

- **Empowering and Motivating:** It increases confidence, improves decision-making, and a sense of purpose.

Overthinking:

- **Repetitive and Cyclical:** Overthinking involves dwelling on the same thoughts and worries without resolution.

- **Negative and Self-Critical:** It focuses on past mistakes, potential future failures, and self-doubt.

- **Based on Fear and Uncertainty:** It often stems from anxiety and a need for control.

- **Debilitating and Exhausting:** It drains energy, hinders decision-making, and increases stress and anxiety.

Understanding the difference between overthinking and healthy thinking is crucial for recognizing when our thoughts become unproductive and counterproductive.

Why Understanding Overthinking Matters

The first step to overcoming any challenge is to understand its nature. Recognizing the characteristics, origins, and consequences of overthinking gives us valuable insights into our mental processes. This self-awareness allows us to identify the triggers, thought patterns, and behaviors contributing to overthinking.

Understanding the overthinking mind empowers us to challenge negative thoughts, develop healthier coping mechanisms, and cultivate a more balanced perspective. It is the foundation upon which we can build strategies to reclaim control of our thoughts, reduce stress and anxiety, and ultimately live a more fulfilling life.

The Overthinking Cycle: How Worry Feeds Itself

Overthinking is not merely a series of random, unwelcome thoughts. It's a complex, self-sustaining process that can be broken down into distinct stages, each feeding into the next. Understanding this cycle is crucial for breaking free from its grasp.

Stage 1: The Trigger:

Every cycle of overthinking begins with a trigger—an event, a conversation, a memory, or even a fleeting thought. It could be a minor setback at work, a comment from a friend, or simply the realization that you forgot to buy milk on your way home. For an overthinker, these triggers are like sparks igniting a tinderbox of thoughts.

Stage 2: The Thought Spiral:

Once the trigger has been pulled, the mind embarks on a relentless journey of analysis and interpretation. The initial thought gives birth to a series of related thoughts, each one more negative and distressing than the last. "What if I fail?" "Why did they say that?" "Am I good enough?" These questions echo endlessly, their answers always seeming to confirm the worst fears.

Stage 3: Emotional Amplification:

As the negative thoughts intensify, so do the emotions they evoke. Anxiety, fear, anger, sadness—these feelings surge through the body, further fueling the thought spiral. The overthinkers become trapped in a negative vortex, their emotions feeding off their thoughts and vice versa.

Stage 4: Behavioral Consequences:

The emotional turmoil of overthinking doesn't remain confined to the mind. It spills over into behavior, often in unproductive or self-destructive ways. The overthinker might withdraw from social interactions, neglect responsibilities, or engage in unhealthy coping mechanisms like excessive eating or substance abuse. These behaviors, in turn, reinforce the negative thoughts and emotions, perpetuating the cycle.

Stage 5: Reinforcement of Beliefs:

Each cycle of overthinking solidifies the underlying beliefs that drive it. If the overthinker's thoughts center on their perceived inadequacies, the cycle reinforces those feelings of insecurity. If the thoughts revolve around the fear of failure, the cycle amplifies that fear. The overthinker's mind becomes a self-fulfilling prophecy, confirming their worst fears and doubts.

The Role of Cognitive Biases and Underlying Fears

While the overthinking cycle is a universal phenomenon, its specific content and intensity vary from person to person. This variation is shaped by cognitive biases—systematic errors in thinking—and underlying fears that lurk beneath the surface.

Cognitive Biases: These are mental shortcuts that help us process information quickly but can also lead us astray. Some common cognitive biases that contribute to overthinking include:

- **Catastrophizing:** Exaggerating the likelihood or severity of negative outcomes.

- **Personalization:** Assuming that events are directly related to oneself when they may not be.

- **Mind Reading:** Believing that we know what others are thinking without sufficient evidence.

- **Filtering:** Focusing on negative details while ignoring positive ones.

Underlying Fears: These are the deep-seated anxieties that drive overthinking. They often stem from childhood experiences, past traumas, or societal conditioning. Some common underlying fears include:

- **Fear of failure:** The belief that we are not good enough and will inevitably fail.

- **Fear of rejection:** The fear of being disliked, abandoned, or excluded.

- **Fear of the unknown:** The anxiety caused by uncertainty and lack of control.

These cognitive biases and underlying fears act as fuel for the overthinking cycle. They distort our perception of reality, amplify negative emotions, and reinforce the beliefs that keep us trapped. Understanding these underlying forces is crucial for breaking free from the cycle and reclaiming our mental peace.

Breaking the Cycle: A Path to Freedom

The overthinking cycle is a formidable opponent, but it is not invincible. By understanding its mechanics, recognizing our cognitive biases, and addressing our underlying fears, we can gradually dismantle the cycle and cultivate a calmer, more balanced mind. The following chapters will explore practical strategies for breaking free from overthinking and reclaiming our mental well-being.

Self-Reflection Questions:

1. **Overthinking Patterns:** When and where do you find yourself overthinking the most? Are there specific triggers or situations that seem to set off this habit?

2. **Worry Themes:** What are the common themes or topics that occupy your thoughts when you overthink? Are you often dwelling on the past, worrying about the future, or fixating on uncertainties?

3. **Emotional Impact:** How does overthinking affect you emotionally? Do you experience anxiety, stress, or a

sense of overwhelm? Does it impact your sleep or overall well-being?

4. **Physical Sensations:** What physical sensations do you notice when you're caught in an overthinking cycle? Do you experience muscle tension, headaches, or changes in your breathing patterns?

5. **Root Causes:** What might be some of the underlying reasons for your overthinking? Are there any past experiences, beliefs, or fears that contribute to this habit?

Transformative Exercises:

1. **Thought Journaling:** Set aside time each day to write down your thoughts and worries. This can help you gain clarity and identify recurring patterns in your thinking.

2. **Mindfulness Meditation:** Practice mindfulness meditation to cultivate present-moment awareness. This can help you break free from the cycle of overthinking and cultivate a calmer, more focused mind.

3. **"What If" Challenge:** When you catch yourself overthinking, challenge your worries with "what if" questions. Instead of focusing on worst-case scenarios, ask yourself, "What if things turn out better than expected?" or "What if I have the strength to handle whatever comes my way?"

4. **Thought Stopping:** When you notice yourself overthinking, say "stop" out loud or in your head. This

can interrupt the thought pattern and create space for more positive or productive thinking.

5. **Body Scan:** When overthinking leads to physical tension, do a body scan meditation. Focus your attention on each part of your body, noticing any sensations of tightness or discomfort. Gently release tension as you breathe deeply.

CHAPTER 2: THE STRESS CONNECTION

"Stress is not what happens to us. It's our response to what happens. And RESPONSE is something we can choose." – Maureen Killoran.

The mind, a marvel of evolution, is capable of extraordinary feats. Yet, when left unchecked, it can become a relentless tormentor. Overthinking, that incessant whirring of thoughts, often acts as the catalyst for an unwelcome guest: stress.

Imagine your mind as a high-powered engine, constantly revving, even when the car is parked. The fuel? Your worries, doubts, and endless "what ifs." This excessive mental activity isn't just exhausting; it triggers a cascade of physiological responses that can wreak havoc on your body and mind.

When you overthink, your brain perceives a threat, even if it's merely a perceived one. This triggers the "fight-or-flight" response, an ancient survival mechanism to protect you from danger. In this state, your body releases stress hormones like cortisol and adrenaline. These hormones prepare you to confront the threat or flee from it, increasing your heart rate, blood pressure, and breathing rate.

While this response is invaluable in life-or-death situations, it becomes problematic when it's chronically activated by overthinking. Imagine living in a constant state of alert, your body primed for battle even when there's no enemy in sight. This is the reality for many overthinkers.

The physiological effects of stress are far-reaching. It can weaken your immune system, making you more susceptible to illness. It can disrupt your sleep, leaving you tired and irritable. Chronic stress can even contribute to serious health conditions, such as heart disease, high blood pressure, and diabetes.

But the damage doesn't stop there. Stress also takes a toll on your mental health. It can lead to anxiety, depression, and burnout. Overthinking can amplify these conditions, creating a vicious cycle where stress fuels overthinking, and overthinking intensifies stress.

Overthinking and stress can also impair your cognitive function. It can make concentrating, remembering things, and making decisions difficult. You may struggle to focus at work or school, and your creativity and problem-solving abilities may suffer.

The emotional toll of stress is equally significant. You may experience mood swings, irritability, and a loss of enjoyment in activities you once loved. Stress can also strain your relationships, as you may withdraw from loved ones or lash out in frustration.

Overthinkers often find themselves trapped in a mental maze of their own creation. They may ruminate over past mistakes, worry about future events, or endlessly analyze social interactions. This mental churning not only fuels stress but also prevents them from enjoying the present moment.

The good news is that you don't have to remain a prisoner of overthinking and stress. By understanding the connection between the two, you can begin to break the cycle and reclaim your peace of mind.

The Overthinking-Stress Connection: A Vicious Cycle of Worry and Weariness

Our minds are incredible tools, capable of creativity, problem-solving, and deep reflection. However, like any tool, they can be misused. When we dwell excessively on problems, replay past events, or worry endlessly about the future, we fall into the trap of overthinking. While seemingly harmless, this mental habit has a profound and often underestimated impact on our stress levels.

How Overthinking Hijacks Your Stress Response

Remember our car engine illustration?. A little revving is normal, but the engine overheats when you keep your foot on the gas pedal for too long. Similarly, overthinking pushes your brain into overdrive, triggering a cascade of physiological reactions that constitute the stress response.

The stress response is an ancient survival mechanism designed to protect us from threats. When we perceive danger, our brains release a flood of stress hormones, primarily cortisol and adrenaline. These hormones prepare our bodies to fight or flee, increasing heart rate, blood pressure, and breathing while diverting resources away from non-essential functions like digestion and immune response.

In the face of a real threat, this response is adaptive. However, overthinking often activates the stress response in the absence of any immediate danger. When we worry about a work presentation, ruminate on a past argument, or obsess over a health concern, our brains interpret these thoughts as threats, even though they may be purely hypothetical. This leads to a chronic activation of the stress response, keeping our bodies and minds in a constant state of high alert.

The Cortisol Connection: Overthinking's Chemical Culprit

One of the key players in this overthinking-stress connection is cortisol. Often called the "stress hormone," cortisol is essential for our survival. However, it wreaks havoc on our well-being when it's chronically elevated due to overthinking.

Elevated cortisol levels have been linked to a wide range of physical and mental health problems, including:

- **Weakened Immune System:** Cortisol suppresses the immune system, making us more susceptible to infections and illnesses. Have you ever noticed that you tend to get sick after intense stress or worry? This is likely due to the impact of cortisol on your immune defenses.

- **Increased Blood Pressure and Heart Rate:** Chronic stress, fueled by overthinking, can contribute to high blood pressure and cardiovascular disease. If you find yourself with a racing heart or pounding headache after a worry session, it's a sign that your stress response is in overdrive.

- **Disrupted Sleep:** Cortisol interferes with sleep patterns, making falling and staying asleep harder. Overthinkers often struggle with insomnia, as their minds continue to race even when their bodies crave rest.

- **Digestive Problems:** Stress can lead to a variety of digestive issues, including irritable bowel syndrome (IBS), stomach ulcers, and acid reflux. If you experience stomach upset or discomfort when you're feeling stressed, overthinking is likely playing a role.

- **Mood Swings and Depression:** Elevated cortisol levels can disrupt the balance of neurotransmitters in the brain, contributing to mood swings, irritability, and even depression. Overthinkers often find themselves caught in a downward spiral of negative emotions fueled by their persistent worries.

Overthinking in Action: Real-Life Stress Triggers

Overthinking can be triggered by a wide range of big and small situations. Here are a few common examples:

- **Work Stress:** Deadlines, presentations, difficult colleagues, and job insecurity can all fuel overthinking. You might find yourself lying awake at night, worrying about an upcoming meeting or replaying a conversation with your boss over and over in your head.

- **Relationship Worries:** Conflicts with partners, family members, or friends can trigger a cascade of anxious thoughts. You might overanalyze text messages, dissect conversations, or worry endlessly about the future of your relationship.

- **Health Concerns:** Even minor health issues can become magnified in the mind of an overthinker. A headache might be interpreted as a sign of a brain tumor or a cough as the onset of a severe illness.

- **Financial Stress:** Money worries can keep you up at night as you fret about bills, debt, or future financial security. You might find yourself constantly checking your bank balance or overthinking every purchase.

These are just a few examples of how overthinking can infiltrate our lives and trigger the stress response. It's important to remember that everyone experiences stress differently, and what triggers overthinking for one person may not affect another.

The Physiological Impact: How Stress Wreaks Havoc on Your Body and Mind

When your mind is racing with worries and "what ifs," it's not just your mental state that suffers – your body also bears the brunt of the burden. Chronic stress, fueled by overthinking, leaves a trail of physical symptoms that can significantly impact your quality of life. Let's explore how overthinking wreaks havoc on various bodily systems:

Sleepless Nights and Exhausted Days: The Toll on Sleep

A good night's sleep is essential for physical and mental restoration. However, overthinking often disrupts this vital process. As you lie in bed, your mind may replay past events, anticipate future challenges, or simply churn with a jumble of anxious thoughts. This mental chatter can make it difficult to fall asleep, stay asleep, or experience restful sleep.

The stress hormone cortisol, elevated during overthinking periods, further exacerbates sleep problems. Cortisol naturally decreases at night, preparing your body for rest. But when you're caught in a cycle of worry, cortisol levels remain high, keeping you alert and wired. This can lead to insomnia, fatigue, and a general feeling of exhaustion that permeates your waking hours.

The Impact on Digestion

Have you ever experienced butterflies in your stomach before a big presentation or felt nauseous during a stressful situation? This is because the gut and the brain are intimately connected, communicating through a complex network of nerves, hormones, and neurotransmitters.

When you're stressed and overthinking, this gut-brain axis can go haywire. Stress hormones can disrupt the balance of gut bacteria, impair digestion, and increase intestinal permeability (leaky gut). This can lead to a variety of digestive problems, including:

- **Irritable Bowel Syndrome (IBS):** This common condition is characterized by abdominal pain, bloating, diarrhea, and constipation. Stress is a well-known trigger for IBS flare-ups.

- **Stomach Ulcers:** While ulcers are primarily caused by a bacteria called H. pylori, stress can worsen symptoms and slow healing.

- **Acid Reflux:** Stress can relax the lower esophageal sphincter (LES), allowing stomach acid to flow back into the esophagus, causing heartburn and discomfort.

A Weakened Shield: The Impact on Immune Function

When you're constantly stressed and overthinking, your immune system takes a hit. The stress hormone cortisol suppresses immune function, making you more susceptible to infections and illnesses. Studies have shown that people who are chronically stressed have a higher risk of catching colds, the flu, and other infections.

Moreover, stress can impair the body's ability to heal. If you've ever noticed that a minor cut or scrape takes longer to recover when you're under stress, it's because your immune system is not functioning optimally.

A Racing Heart and Rising Pressure: The Impact on Cardiovascular Health

Chronic stress is a major risk factor for cardiovascular disease. When you're overthinking, your heart rate and blood pressure increase, putting a strain on your heart and blood vessels. Over time, this can lead to:

- **High Blood Pressure:** Chronic stress can contribute to the development of hypertension, which increases the risk of heart attack, stroke, and other cardiovascular problems.

- **Atherosclerosis:** Stress can promote the buildup of plaque in the arteries, narrowing them and reducing blood flow to the heart and other organs.

- **Heart Attack and Stroke:** In severe cases, chronic stress can trigger a heart attack or stroke.

The Ripple Effect: Overthinking's Impact on Overall Well-being

The physical effects of overthinking extend beyond individual organs and systems. Chronic stress can lead to a general decline in overall well-being, affecting your energy levels, mood, and quality of life. You may experience:

- **Fatigue and Exhaustion:** Constant worry and mental strain can leave you feeling drained and depleted, even if you're getting enough sleep.

- **Weight Gain or Loss:** Stress can affect appetite and metabolism, leading to changes in weight. Some people overeat when stressed, while others lose their appetite.

- **Chronic Pain:** Stress can exacerbate existing pain conditions or trigger new ones. Muscle tension, headaches, and backaches are common complaints among those who are chronically stressed.

- **Skin Problems:** Stress can worsen skin conditions like acne, eczema, and psoriasis.

- **Hair Loss:** In some cases, extreme stress can lead to hair loss.

The Long-Term Risks: Chronic Stress and Disease

While the short-term effects of stress are unpleasant enough, the long-term consequences can be even more dire. Chronic stress has been linked to an increased risk of:

- **Cardiovascular Disease:** As mentioned earlier, stress is a major risk factor for heart attack, stroke, and other cardiovascular problems.

- **Diabetes:** Stress can disrupt blood sugar regulation, increasing the risk of developing type 2 diabetes.

- **Obesity:** Chronic stress can contribute to weight gain and obesity, which in turn, increases the risk of various health problems.

- **Autoimmune Diseases:** Stress may play a role in developing autoimmune diseases, in which the immune system attacks the body's tissues.

- **Mental Health Disorders:** Chronic stress can increase the risk of developing or worsening anxiety disorders, depression, and other mental health conditions.

1. **Stress Signals:** How does stress manifest in your body? Do you experience physical symptoms like muscle tension, headaches, or fatigue? What about mental or emotional signs like irritability, difficulty concentrating, or feelings of overwhelm?

2. **Stress Coping Mechanisms:** What do you currently do to manage stress? Are these strategies healthy and effective? Do they help you address the root causes of stress, or are they merely temporary Band-Aids?

3. **Stressful Thoughts:** What are some of the common thoughts or worries that contribute to your stress? Are these thoughts based on reality, or are they fueled by fear and anxiety?

4. **Stress-Focus Connection:** How does stress affect your ability to focus? Do you find it harder to concentrate when you're feeling stressed? How does this impact your productivity and goal attainment?

Transformative Exercises:

1. **Mindful Breathing:** Practice deep, mindful breathing exercises for 5-10 minutes daily. Focus on the sensation of your breath entering and leaving your body, letting go of distracting thoughts and worries. This can help calm your nervous system and reduce stress levels.

2. **Body Scan Meditation:** Lie down or sit comfortably and systematically bring your attention to different parts

of your body. Notice any areas of tension or discomfort, and consciously relax those muscles. This can help you become more aware of the physical manifestations of stress and release pent-up tension.

3. **Stress-Relieving Activities:** Incorporate activities into your routine that promote relaxation and stress reduction. This could include exercise, spending time in nature, listening to calming music, or engaging in hobbies you enjoy.

4. **Cognitive Reappraisal:** When faced with a stressful situation, try to reframe your perspective. Instead of seeing it as a threat, view it as a challenge or an opportunity for growth. This can help shift your emotional response and reduce the impact of stress.

CHAPTER 3: TAMING THE ANXIETY BEAST

"Anxiety does not empty tomorrow of its sorrows, but only empties today of its strength." - Charles Spurgeon.

The quote above perfectly encapsulates the destructive power of anxiety, a relentless force that can rob us of our present joy and leave us feeling drained and defeated.

Anxiety disorders are the most common mental illness in the world, affecting millions of people. In the United States alone, an estimated 40 million adults suffer from some form of anxiety. It's a pervasive issue that can manifest in various ways, from persistent worry and restlessness to debilitating panic attacks. But, many people don't realize that overthinking often plays a significant role in fueling and exacerbating these anxious feelings.

Think of your mind as a magnifying glass. When you focus on a problem or worry, your mind can magnify it, making it seem more extensive and more threatening than it is. Overthinking acts like a magnifying glass on steroids, amplifying every fear, doubt, and insecurity until they feel overwhelming. This can lead to a vicious cycle where anxiety triggers overthinking, and overthinking further intensifies anxiety.

For individuals already predisposed to anxiety, overthinking can be like pouring gasoline on a fire. It can exacerbate existing symptoms and make them harder to manage. For example, someone with generalized anxiety disorder (GAD) might find that their worries become more frequent and intense when they engage in overthinking. Similarly, someone with social anxiety disorder (SAD) might ruminate on social interactions, magnifying their fears of judgment and rejection.

But overthinking isn't just a problem for those with pre-existing anxiety. In some cases, it can actually be the catalyst for developing an anxiety disorder. When we constantly dwell on negative thoughts and worst-case scenarios, we train our brains to be hypervigilant and to perceive threats where none may exist. This can lead to new anxieties or the worsening of existing ones.

One of the most common ways overthinking fuels anxiety is through a process called catastrophizing. This is when we blow a relatively minor problem out of proportion, imagining the worst possible outcome. For example, a minor disagreement with a friend might be interpreted as a sign that the friendship is doomed, or a missed deadline at work might be seen as a career-ending failure.

Another way overthinking contributes to anxiety is through rumination. This is the tendency to dwell on negative thoughts and emotions, replaying them repeatedly in our minds. Rumination can be like a broken record, constantly playing the same negative track until it becomes ingrained in our thinking patterns. This can lead to a sense of hopelessness and despair, making it difficult to break free from the cycle of anxiety.

Overthinking can also lead to a state of hyperarousal, where our bodies are constantly on high alert. This can manifest as physical symptoms like a racing heart, shallow breathing, muscle tension, and difficulty sleeping. Mentally, it can lead to difficulty concentrating, irritability, and a feeling of being constantly on edge.

It's important to understand that anxiety is not a one-size-fits-all condition. There are different types of anxiety disorders, each with its own unique set of symptoms. Some of the most common include:

- **Generalized Anxiety Disorder (GAD):** This is characterized by excessive and persistent worry about a variety of things, such as work, health, relationships, or finances. People with GAD often feel like they can't control their worry, and it interferes with their daily lives.

- **Panic Disorder:** This involves sudden and unexpected panic attacks, which are intense episodes of fear accompanied by physical symptoms like heart palpitations, sweating, trembling, and shortness of breath. People with panic disorder often live in fear of having another attack.

- **Social Anxiety Disorder (SAD):** This is characterized by an intense fear of social situations and scrutiny from others. People with SAD may avoid social gatherings, worry excessively about being judged or embarrassed, and experience physical symptoms like blushing and sweating in social settings.

While these are some of the most common anxiety disorders, there are many other types, including specific phobias (e.g., fear of flying, spiders, or heights) and obsessive-compulsive disorder (OCD). Each disorder has unique symptoms and challenges, but overthinking is often a common thread that runs through them all.

Overthinking and Anxiety: Fueling the Flames of Fear

Anxiety is a natural human emotion, a response to perceived threats or uncertainties. It can be a helpful signal, alerting us to potential dangers and motivating us to take action. However, when anxiety becomes excessive, persistent, and disproportionate to the actual situation, it can be debilitating. Overthinking plays a significant role in fueling the flames of anxiety, turning manageable worries into raging infernos of fear.

The Mind's Magnifying Glass: How Overthinking Amplifies Anxiety

Imagine your mind as a magnifying glass. When you focus it on a small object, the object appears larger and more significant. Similarly, overthinking amplifies our anxieties, making them seem bigger and more threatening than they truly are.

One way overthinking fuels anxiety is through a process called catastrophic thinking. This involves imagining the worst-case scenario in a given situation, often blowing things out of proportion. For example, a minor setback at work might be interpreted as a sign of impending failure, or a disagreement with a friend might be seen as the end of the relationship.

Another way overthinking contributes to anxiety is through rumination. This is the tendency to dwell on negative thoughts and experiences, replaying them repeatedly in our minds. Rumination keeps our focus on problems and prevents us from moving forward. It can also lead to a downward spiral of negativity, as one anxious thought triggers another.

"What If" Scenarios: The Anxiety-Provoking Power of Uncertainty

Overthinking also thrives on uncertainty. When we don't have all the information or can't predict the future, our minds tend to fill in the gaps with worst-case scenarios. These "what if" scenarios are often based on fear and irrational beliefs but can feel very real and threatening.

For example, if you're waiting for medical test results, you might find yourself asking, "What if it's cancer?" or "What if I have a serious illness?" Even though there may be no evidence to support these fears, they can generate a tremendous amount of anxiety.

The Illusion of Control: Overthinking as a Coping Mechanism

Why do we overthink? Often, it's a misguided attempt to gain control over a situation. If we analyze every detail, anticipate every possibility, and worry about every potential outcome, we can somehow prevent bad things from happening.

However, this illusion of control is just that – an illusion. In reality, overthinking often makes us feel more anxious and powerless. It's like trying to control the weather by obsessing over the forecast. The weather will do what it's going to do, regardless of how much we worry about it.

The Role of Uncertainty in Anxiety

Uncertainty is a fundamental part of life. We can't predict the future and don't always have all the information we need to make decisions. This lack of control can be a major source of anxiety for overthinkers.

When we're faced with uncertainty, our minds tend to go into overdrive, trying to find answers and solutions. This can lead to a cycle of worry, rumination, and catastrophic thinking. The more we try to control the uncontrollable, the more anxious we become.

Recognizing the Patterns: Real-Life Examples of Overthinking and Anxiety

To better understand how overthinking fuels anxiety, let's look at some real-life examples:

- **Social Anxiety:** Before a social event, an overthinker might spend hours worrying about what to wear, what to say, and how they will be perceived. They might imagine embarrassing themselves or being rejected by others. This can lead to intense anxiety and even avoidance of social situations.

- **Performance Anxiety:** A student preparing for an exam might overanalyze every detail of the material, worrying about forgetting information or making mistakes. They might spend so much time worrying that they neglect their studies, further fueling their anxiety.

- **Health Anxiety:** Someone with health anxiety might obsess over minor symptoms, fearing that they have a serious illness. They might spend hours researching their symptoms online, which often leads to more worry and anxiety.

Anxiety's Many Faces: Recognizing the Symptoms and Finding Relief

Anxiety is not a one-size-fits-all experience. It can manifest in various ways, each with unique symptoms and challenges. Understanding the different types of anxiety disorders is crucial for recognizing when you or someone you care about might need help. Let's delve into three common anxiety disorders: Generalized Anxiety Disorder (GAD), Social Anxiety Disorder (SAD), and Panic Disorder.

Generalized Anxiety Disorder (GAD): The Worry That Never Rests

If you've ever felt like worry is your constant companion, you might be familiar with GAD. People with GAD experience excessive and persistent worry about a wide range of topics, such as work, health, finances, or relationships. This worry feels uncontrollable and often out of proportion to the actual situation.

Physical Symptoms of GAD:

- **Muscle tension and headaches:** Ever felt like your shoulders are permanently glued to your ears? GAD can manifest as chronic muscle tension, often leading to headaches and body aches.

- **Fatigue and difficulty sleeping:** Worrying all the time is exhausting! GAD can disrupt sleep patterns, leaving you feeling tired and drained even after a whole night's rest.

- **Stomach problems and nausea:** Butterflies in your stomach can be more than just a sign of excitement. GAD can trigger digestive issues like stomachaches, nausea, and diarrhea.

Emotional and Cognitive Symptoms of GAD:

- **Restlessness and irritability:** It's hard to relax when your mind is racing. GAD can make you feel constantly on edge, irritable, and unable to unwind.

- **Difficulty concentrating:** When worry consumes your thoughts, it's hard to focus on anything else. GAD can make completing tasks, following conversations, or even enjoying your favorite activities challenging.

- **Feeling overwhelmed and on edge:** The weight of constant worry can feel crushing. GAD can leave you feeling overwhelmed, helpless, and unable to cope with everyday challenges.

Social Anxiety Disorder (SAD): The Fear of Social Judgment

If social situations fill you with dread, you might be dealing with SAD. People with SAD experience intense fear and anxiety in social settings, fearing judgment, scrutiny, or embarrassment.

Physical Symptoms of SAD:

- **Blushing and sweating:** Have you ever felt your cheeks flush or your palms sweat during a social interaction? SAD can trigger these physical reactions, further fueling feelings of self-consciousness.

- **Racing heart and trembling:** The mere thought of a social gathering can send your heart into overdrive. SAD can manifest as physical symptoms that mirror a panic attack.

- **Upset stomach and nausea:** Social anxiety can be a real gut-wrenching experience. SAD often causes digestive problems like nausea, diarrhea, or constipation.

Emotional and Cognitive Symptoms of SAD:

- **Intense fear of being judged or embarrassed:** This is the hallmark of SAD. The fear of negative evaluation can be so overwhelming that it leads to avoidance of social situations altogether.

- **Difficulty talking to strangers:** Initiating conversations or speaking in front of others can feel like an insurmountable challenge for people with SAD.

- **Feeling self-conscious and inadequate:** SAD often goes hand in hand with low self-esteem and negative self-talk. This can create a vicious cycle of social anxiety and self-doubt.

Panic Disorder: The Storm of Sudden Fear

Panic disorder is characterized by sudden and recurrent panic attacks. A panic attack is an intense wave of fear that peaks within minutes and includes physical symptoms like a racing heart, shortness of breath, and dizziness.

Physical Symptoms of Panic Disorder:

- **Racing or pounding heart:** During a panic attack, your heart might feel like it's about to jump out of your chest. This can be extremely frightening and contribute to feelings of impending doom.

- **Sweating and trembling:** Your body goes into fight-or-flight mode during a panic attack, triggering physical reactions like sweating and shaking.

- **Shortness of breath or feeling smothered:** It can feel like you're not getting enough air, further intensifying the fear and panic.

Emotional and Cognitive Symptoms of Panic Disorder:

- **Intense fear of dying or losing control:** Panic attacks can be so overwhelming that they create a sense of impending doom. You might feel like you're having a heart attack or going crazy.

- **Feeling detached from reality (derealization):** During a panic attack, you might feel like you're in a dream or watching yourself from outside your body.

- **Fear of future panic attacks:** The anticipation of another panic attack can lead to avoidance behaviors and a constant state of anxiety.

Recognizing the Signs and Seeking Help

Anxiety disorders are not a sign of weakness or a character flaw. They are real medical conditions that can be effectively treated with therapy, medication, or both.

If you or someone you know is experiencing any of the symptoms described above, seeking professional help is important. A doctor or mental health professional can conduct an evaluation and recommend the most appropriate treatment options.

Tips for Recognizing Anxiety:

- Pay attention to your body: Notice any physical symptoms that arise in certain situations or without apparent cause.

- Monitor your thoughts: Are you frequently worrying, overthinking, or catastrophizing?

- Observe your behavior: Do you avoid certain situations due to fear or anxiety?

Seeking Help:

- Talk to your doctor or a mental health professional.

- Consider therapy, such as cognitive-behavioral therapy (CBT), which can help you identify and change negative thought patterns.

- If recommended, medication can help manage anxiety symptoms.

Remember, you are not alone. Millions of people struggle with anxiety disorders. With the proper support and treatment, you can overcome anxiety and live a full and fulfilling life.

Self-Reflection Questions:

1. **Anxiety Triggers:** What specific situations, events, or thoughts trigger your anxiety? Are there any patterns or commonalities among these triggers?

2. **Anxiety Symptoms:** How does anxiety manifest in your body? Do you experience physical sensations like rapid heartbeat, shortness of breath, or muscle tension? How does it affect your thoughts and behaviors?

3. **Coping Mechanisms:** What strategies do you currently use to manage anxiety and overthinking? Are these

strategies healthy and effective, or do they sometimes exacerbate the problem?

4. **Anxiety's Impact:** How does anxiety affect your daily life? Does it interfere with your relationships, work, or overall well-being? What aspects of your life would you like to improve by managing your anxiety better?

Transformative Exercises:

1. **Thought Challenging:** When you catch yourself overthinking or engaging in catastrophic thinking, challenge those thoughts with evidence and logic. Ask yourself, "Is this really likely to happen? What's the worst that could happen, and how would I cope with it?"

2. **Worry Journaling:** Set aside a specific time each day to write down your worries and anxieties. This can help you externalize them and gain a clearer perspective. Afterward, try engaging in a relaxing activity to redirect your focus.

3. **Grounding Techniques:** When anxiety strikes, use grounding techniques to bring yourself back to the present. Focus on your senses—what do you see, hear, smell, taste, and touch? This can help you anchor yourself and reduce the overwhelming feeling of anxiety.

4. **Self-Compassion:** Practice self-compassion when you experience anxiety. Recognize that it's a common human experience and that you're not alone in your

struggles. Treat yourself with kindness and understanding, just as you would a friend in a similar situation.

CHAPTER 4: DECLUTTER YOUR MIND

Ever felt like your mind is a browser with too many tabs open? That buzzing, chaotic feeling of too many thoughts vying for your attention? It's not just you. Research shows that the average person has 6,200 thoughts per day. That's a lot of mental traffic!

But just like a cluttered desk makes it hard to focus, a cluttered mind makes it difficult to find peace, make decisions, or enjoy the present moment. This is where decluttering your mind comes in – creating mental space and clarity.

Think of it like spring cleaning for your brain. Just as you'd tidy up your living space to make it more inviting and functional, decluttering your mind can create a sense of calm, focus, and well-being. It's about letting go of the mental baggage that weighs you down to move forward with greater ease and joy.

Why is decluttering your mind so important? For starters, it can help you manage stress and anxiety. When your mind is filled with worries, regrets, and to-do lists, it's hard to relax and be present. But when you clear away the mental clutter, you create space for peace and tranquility.

A decluttered mind also enhances your creativity and problem-solving abilities. You're more likely to develop innovative ideas and solutions when a million thoughts do not bog you down. It's like clearing the weeds from a garden – the flowers can bloom once the distractions are gone.

Decluttering your mind isn't about suppressing your thoughts or pretending they don't exist. It's about acknowledging, processing, and then letting them go. This allows you to focus on what truly matters in the present rather than getting caught up in the past or worrying about the future.

So, how do you go about decluttering your mind? You can use many different techniques, and the best approach will vary from person to person. But one of the most powerful tools for decluttering your mind is mindfulness.

Mindfulness is simply paying attention to the present moment without judgment. It's about being aware of your thoughts, feelings, and sensations as they arise without getting caught up in them. When you practice mindfulness, you create a space between yourself and your thoughts, which allows you to observe them with greater clarity and detachment.

This sense of detachment is vital to decluttering your mind. When you can observe your thoughts without getting entangled, you're less likely to be swept away by their emotional currents. You can choose which thoughts to engage with and which to let go.

Mindfulness can be practiced in many different ways. You can meditate, do yoga, walk in nature, or focus on your breath for a few minutes. The key is to find a practice that works for you and to make it a regular part of your routine.

Mindfulness isn't the only tool for decluttering your mind, but it's powerful. By cultivating present-moment awareness, you can reduce the mental chatter, create space for peace and clarity, and live a more fulfilling life.

Thought Dumping: Clearing the Mental Clutter

What is Thought Dumping?

Thought dumping is like taking out the mental trash. It's a simple process of writing down all the thoughts swirling around in your head without judgment or censorship. It's like opening the floodgates of your mind and letting everything pour onto the page. The idea is to get those thoughts out of your head and onto paper (or a digital document), where you can see them more clearly and objectively.

Why Thought Dumping Works

You might wonder, "How can simply writing down my thoughts make a difference?" Well, there are several reasons why thought dumping is so effective:

1. **Releases Pent-up Emotions:** When we keep our thoughts bottled up, they can fester and intensify. By writing them down, we give ourselves permission to express and acknowledge our emotions, whether they're positive or negative. This can be incredibly cathartic and lead to a sense of relief.

2. **Creates Mental Space:** Our minds have a limited capacity for holding information. When we're constantly juggling thoughts and worries, it can feel like our brains are about to explode. Thought dumping frees

up mental space, allowing us to think more clearly and focus on the present moment.

3. **Clarity and Perspective:** Seeing our thoughts on paper (or screen) allows us to examine them more objectively. We can identify patterns, recurring themes, and even irrational or unhelpful thought patterns. This newfound clarity can help us make better decisions and take more effective action.

4. **Reduces Overthinking and Rumination:** Overthinking often involves replaying the same thoughts repeatedly, like a broken record. Thought dumping can help break this cycle by externalizing those thoughts and giving our minds a break.

How to Do a Thought Dump: A Step-by-Step Guide

Ready to declutter your mind? Here's how to do a thought dump:

1. **Find a Quiet Space:** Choose a place you won't be interrupted. This could be your bedroom, a cozy corner of your home, or even a park bench if you enjoy being outdoors.

2. **Gather Your Tools:** Grab a notebook and pen, or open a blank document on your computer or phone.

3. **Set a Timer:** If you're new to thought dumping, set a timer for 5-10 minutes. This will help you stay focused and prevent you from getting overwhelmed.

4. **Start Writing:** Write down everything that comes to mind. Don't worry about grammar, spelling, or whether your thoughts make sense. Just let the words flow freely. Here are some prompts to get you started:

   - *"What am I worried about right now?"*

   - *"What's been on my mind lately?"*

   - *"What tasks do I need to get done?"*

   - *"What emotions am I feeling?"*

   - *"What am I grateful for?"*

5. **Don't Edit or Judge:** Resist the urge to censor yourself or judge your thoughts. Remember, this is a safe space for you to express whatever is on your mind.

6. **Keep Going:** Continue writing until the timer goes off or until you feel like you've emptied your mind.

7. **Review (Optional):** After your thought dump, you can review what you've written. Look for patterns, insights, or any action steps you can take to address your concerns.

Tips for Effective Thought Dumping

- **Make it a Habit:** The more you practice thought dumping, the more natural it will become. Try doing it daily, weekly, or whenever you feel mentally overwhelmed.

- **Experiment with Different Formats:** Some people prefer free writing, while others like to use bullet points or mind maps. Find a format that works best for you.

- **Don't Force It:** If you're struggling to come up with thoughts, don't worry. Just start writing anything, even if it's just "I don't know what to write." Sometimes, the act of writing can unlock your thoughts.

- **Be Kind to Yourself:** Remember, thought dumping is not about perfection. It's about giving yourself the space to express your thoughts and emotions without judgment.

Mindfulness and Meditation: Cultivating Present Moment Awareness

Our minds are often consumed by worries about the future or regrets about the past. We get caught in a relentless cycle of thoughts, plans, and anxieties, leaving little room for simply being. Mindfulness and meditation offer a powerful antidote to this constant mental chatter, inviting us to step out of the chaos and into the tranquility of the present moment.

What is Mindfulness?

Mindfulness is the practice of paying full attention to the present moment without judgment. It's about being aware of our thoughts, feelings, bodily sensations, and the world without getting caught up in them. Think of it as hitting the pause button on your mental autopilot and tuning in to the here and now.

What is Meditation?

Meditation is a practice that cultivates mindfulness. It involves focusing on a single point, such as your breath, a mantra, or a visual image. By anchoring your mind in the present, meditation helps to quiet the inner chatter and create a sense of calm and clarity.

The Dynamic Duo: How Mindfulness and Meditation Combat Overthinking

Mindfulness and meditation are like two sides of the same coin, working together to combat the negative effects of overthinking. Here's how:

1. **Increased Awareness:** Mindfulness helps us become more aware of our thought patterns. By observing our thoughts without judgment, we can identify triggers for overthinking and develop strategies for interrupting the cycle.

2. **Reduced Reactivity:** When we're mindful, we're less likely to react impulsively to our thoughts and emotions. Instead of getting swept away by worry or anxiety, we can choose how to respond, creating space for more thoughtful and intentional actions.

3. **Stress Reduction:** Meditation has been shown to lower cortisol levels, the stress hormone. By calming the nervous system, it helps to reduce physical and mental tension, promoting relaxation and well-being.

4. **Improved Focus:** Regular meditation practice can enhance our ability to concentrate and focus. By training our minds to stay present, we become less easily distracted by worries and ruminations.

5. **Emotional Regulation:** Mindfulness and meditation can help us develop a healthier relationship with our emotions. Instead of suppressing or avoiding difficult feelings, we can learn to acknowledge and accept them without judgment, leading to greater emotional balance.

Mindfulness in Action: Simple Exercises for Daily Life

You don't need to be a Zen master to reap the benefits of mindfulness. Here are a few simple exercises you can incorporate into your daily routine:

1. **Mindful Breathing:** Find a quiet place to sit or lie down. Close your eyes or soften your gaze. Focus your attention on your breath as it enters and leaves your body. Notice the rise and fall of your chest or abdomen. If your mind wanders, gently bring it back to your breath. Practice for 5-10 minutes.

2. **Body Scan Meditation:** Lie down or sit comfortably. Close your eyes. Start by focusing on your toes, noticing any sensations you feel. Slowly move your attention up your body, through your feet, legs, torso, arms, and head, paying attention to each body part without judgment. Practice for 10-15 minutes.

3. **Mindful Eating:** Slow down and savor each bite during your next meal. Pay attention to the flavors, textures, and aromas of your food. Notice the sensations of chewing and swallowing. Avoid distractions like TV or your phone.

4. **Mindful Walking:** As you walk, focus on the sensations of your feet touching the ground. Notice the movement of your legs and the feeling of the air on your skin. Pay attention to the sights, sounds, and smells around you.

5. **Mindful Moments:** Throughout your day, pause for a few moments to check in with yourself. Notice your thoughts, feelings, and bodily sensations. Are you tense? Relaxed? Hungry? Tired? Simply acknowledging these sensations without judgment can bring a sense of calm and clarity.

The Journey to a Calmer Mind

Remember, mindfulness and meditation are practices, not quick fixes. Like any skill, they require patience and consistency to see results. Start with a few minutes each day and gradually increase the duration as you become more comfortable.

It's also important to be kind to yourself. Your mind will wander, and that's okay. Gently bring your attention back to the present moment without self-criticism. With regular practice, you'll find that mindfulness and meditation become easier and more enjoyable, leading to a calmer mind, reduced stress, and a greater sense of well-being.

As you continue to cultivate mindfulness, you'll discover that you can access this peaceful state of mind during formal meditation and throughout your day. By embracing the present moment, you can break free from overthinking and live a more vibrant, joyful, and fulfilling life. Remember, the present moment is a gift; mindfulness allows us to unwrap it fully. As you continue to cultivate mindfulness and deepen your meditation practice, you'll find yourself better equipped to navigate life's challenges with grace, resilience, and a renewed sense of calm.

Self-Reflection Questions:

1. **Mental Inventory:** What thoughts, worries, or to-do lists tend to consume your mental energy? Are there recurring themes or patterns that keep resurfacing?

2. **Thought Triggers:** What external factors or situations trigger mental clutter? Do certain environments, interactions, or times of day make it more difficult to focus?

3. **Mental Relaxation:** What strategies do you use to relax and quiet your mind? Do you engage in activities like meditation, deep breathing, or spending time in nature? How effective are these practices for you?

4. **Mental Clarity:** When do you feel most mentally clear and focused? What conditions or circumstances

contribute to this state of mind? How can you create more of these conditions in your daily life?

Transformative Exercises:

1. **Brain Dump:** Set a timer for 10-15 minutes and write down everything that's on your mind, without filtering or editing. This can help you clear mental clutter and create space for more focused thinking.

2. **Mindfulness Check-In:** Throughout the day, pause for a few moments to check in with your thoughts and feelings. Notice any tension or mental chatter, and gently redirect your attention to the present moment.

3. **Guided Meditation:** Experiment with different guided meditations specifically designed for focus and clarity. Apps like Headspace or Calm offer a variety of options to suit your needs and preferences.

4. **Mindful Movement:** Engage in activities that promote mindfulness and body awareness, such as yoga, tai chi, or walking in nature. Pay attention to your senses and the sensations in your body as you move.

CHAPTER 5: REFRAMING NEGATIVE THOUGHTS

"The mind is everything. What you think you become." - Buddha

These words, spoken centuries ago, hold a profound truth that modern science is only beginning to fully understand. Our thoughts are not mere fleeting whispers in our heads; they are powerful forces that shape our emotions, behaviors, and, ultimately, our lives. When we allow negative thoughts to dominate our minds, we create a self-fulfilling prophecy of stress, anxiety, and unhappiness. But when we learn to challenge and reframe these thoughts, we open the door to a world of possibilities.

Consider this: the average person has tens of thousands of thoughts every day. Many of these thoughts are automatic and unconscious, shaped by our past experiences, beliefs, and biases. Unfortunately, for those prone to overthinking, many of these thoughts tend to be negative, self-critical, or worry-ridden.

These negative thoughts are like seeds planted in the fertile soil of our minds. If we water them with attention and belief, they will grow into weeds that choke our happiness and well-being. But if we uproot these weeds and plant seeds of positivity and self-compassion instead, we can cultivate a garden of mental and emotional flourishing.

The good news is that we have the power to choose our thoughts. While we can't always control the initial thoughts that pop into our heads, we can decide how we respond to them. We can choose to believe them or challenge them. We can choose to dwell on them or let them go. We can choose to feed the negative or nourish the positive.

Reframing negative thoughts is like changing how we view the world. Instead of seeing only problems and obstacles, we can start to see opportunities and solutions. We can acknowledge our strengths and potential instead of focusing on our flaws and shortcomings. Instead of dwelling on the past or worrying about the future, we can embrace the present moment and all that it has to offer.

This is not about denying reality or putting on a fake smile. It's about recognizing that our thoughts are not always accurate reflections of reality. It's about challenging our assumptions, questioning our beliefs, and seeking alternative perspectives. It's about cultivating a mindset grounded in reality yet open to possibility.

One of the most powerful tools for reframing negative thoughts is simply pausing and observing them. When you notice a negative thought arising, don't judge it or try to push it away. Instead, acknowledge it with curiosity and compassion. Ask yourself:

- *Is this thought helpful or harmful?*

- *Is it based on facts or feelings?*

- *Is there another way to look at this situation?*

- *What would I say to a friend who was having this thought?*

Observing our thoughts without judgment creates a space for new perspectives to emerge. We can then begin to challenge the negative thoughts and replace them with more positive and realistic ones.

For example, if you find yourself thinking, "I'm such a failure," you might challenge this thought by asking yourself:

- *What evidence do I have to support this thought?*

- *Have I ever succeeded at anything before?*

- *What are my strengths and talents?*

- *What can I learn from this experience?*

By challenging the negative thought and reframing it more positively, you can shift your emotional state and open yourself up to new possibilities.

The Power of Positive Self-Talk: Rewriting Your Inner Narrative for a Calmer Mind

The words we use to talk to ourselves, whether spoken aloud or thought in our minds, profoundly impact our emotions, behaviors, and overall well-being. This inner dialogue, self-talk, can either uplift and empower us or drag us down a spiral of negativity and self-doubt.

Think of your self-talk as a constant stream of commentary running in the background of your mind. The voice evaluates your experiences, judges your actions, and interprets your thoughts. When this voice is kind, supportive, and encouraging, it can boost your confidence, resilience, and motivation. However, when it's critical, judgmental, and pessimistic, it can fuel anxiety, depression, and a host of other mental health problems.

Negative Self-Talk: The Saboteur Within

Negative self-talk is like a relentless critic that finds fault with you and your actions. It can manifest in many forms, including:

- **Self-Criticism:** "I'm so stupid," "I always mess things up," "I'm not good enough."

- **Catastrophizing:** "This is the worst thing that could happen," "I'll never recover from this," "Everything is going to fall apart."

- **Blaming:** "It's all my fault," "I should have known better," "I deserve this."

These negative thoughts can become deeply ingrained patterns, shaping our beliefs about ourselves and our abilities. When we repeatedly tell ourselves that we're not good enough, we start to believe it. This can lead to a vicious cycle of self-doubt, insecurity, and fear of failure.

Overthinking and Anxiety: Fueling the Fire

Negative self-talk is a major contributor to overthinking and anxiety. We create a breeding ground for anxious thoughts and feelings when we constantly criticize ourselves, worry about the future, or ruminate on past mistakes.

For example, if you're preparing for a job interview, negative self-talk might sound like this: "I'm not qualified for this position. I'll probably mess up the interview and embarrass myself. They'll never hire me." These thoughts can trigger a cascade of anxiety, making it difficult to focus, prepare effectively, and perform well in the interview.

Similarly, negative self-talk might escalate your worry if you're dealing with a health concern: "This is probably something serious. What if it's cancer? I'm going to die." These thoughts can send your anxiety levels soaring, making it even harder to cope with the situation.

The Power of Positive Self-Talk: Your Inner Cheerleader

Positive self-talk, on the other hand, is like having a supportive friend or mentor cheering you on. It involves consciously focusing on your strengths, celebrating your successes, and cultivating a more optimistic outlook.

Positive self-talk can take many forms, including:

- **Affirmations:** "I am capable," "I am worthy," "I am enough."

- **Encouragement:** "I can handle this," "I'm making progress," "I'm proud of myself."

- **Realistic Optimism:** "I'll do my best," "I'm learning and growing," "Things will work out."

Replacing negative self-talk with positive affirmations allows you to rewire your brain for resilience, confidence, and inner peace. Positive self-talk helps to:

- **Reduce Stress and Anxiety:** By focusing on the positive, you can calm your nervous system and reduce the production of stress hormones.

- **Boost Confidence:** When you believe in yourself, you're more likely to take risks, pursue your goals, and overcome challenges.

- **Improve Mood:** Positive self-talk can help you cultivate a more optimistic outlook, leading to greater happiness and life satisfaction.

- **Enhance Resilience:** By reminding yourself of your strengths and past successes, you can more easily bounce back from setbacks.

Cultivating Positive Self-Talk: Practical Techniques

Reframing negative thoughts is a skill that takes practice, but it's well worth the effort. Here are some techniques to get you started:

1. **Identify Negative Thoughts:** Pay attention to your inner dialogue throughout the day. When you notice negative thoughts, write them down or mentally note them.

2. **Challenge Negative Thoughts:** Ask yourself if your thoughts are based on facts or fears. Are you catastrophizing or jumping to conclusions? Look for evidence that contradicts your negative beliefs.

3. **Reframe Negative Thoughts:** Replace negative thoughts with more positive and realistic ones. For example, instead of saying, "I'm a failure," try saying, "I'm learning and growing." Instead of saying, "I can't do this," try saying, "I can do this with effort and support."

4. **Practice Positive Affirmations:** Choose affirmations that resonate with you and repeat them to yourself regularly. Write them on sticky notes, set reminders on your phone, or say them aloud in the mirror.

5. **Surround Yourself with Positivity:** Spend time with supportive people who encourage and uplift you. Limit your exposure to negative news and media. Read inspiring books and articles.

6. **Focus on Your Strengths:** List your positive qualities, skills, and accomplishments. Refer to this list when you're feeling down or doubting yourself.

7. **Celebrate Your Successes:** Take the time to acknowledge and appreciate your achievements, no matter how small they may seem.

8. **Practice Self-Compassion:** Be kind to yourself when you make mistakes or experience setbacks. Remember

that everyone makes mistakes, and it's okay not to be perfect.

The Ripple Effect of Positive Self-Talk

The benefits of positive self-talk extend far beyond just reducing overthinking and anxiety. Cultivating a positive inner dialogue creates a ripple effect that positively impacts every aspect of your life.

- **Improved Relationships:** When you feel good about yourself, you're more likely to attract positive and supportive people into your life. You're also more likely to communicate effectively, resolve conflicts peacefully, and build stronger connections with others.

- **Increased Productivity:** Positive self-talk can enhance your motivation, focus, and creativity. Believing in your abilities makes you more likely to take on challenges, persevere through obstacles, and achieve your goals.

- **Enhanced Physical Health:** Research has shown that positive emotions and a positive outlook can boost your immune system, reduce pain, and promote longevity. Positive self-talk can also contribute to better physical health by reducing stress and anxiety.

The Journey to Self-Love and Acceptance

Remember, changing your self-talk takes time and effort. Be patient with yourself, and don't get discouraged if you slip back into negative patterns occasionally. The key is to consistently practice positive self-talk until it becomes a natural part of your inner dialogue.

By focusing on the positive, challenging negative thoughts, and practicing self-compassion, you can rewrite your inner narrative and create a more empowering, joyful, and fulfilling life.

Cognitive Restructuring: Rewiring Your Brain for Positivity and Resilience

We've explored the power of positive self-talk in shifting our inner dialogue, but what if our negative thoughts are deeply ingrained and seem unshakeable? That's where cognitive restructuring, a key technique in cognitive-behavioral therapy (CBT), comes in.

Think of cognitive restructuring as a mental makeover for your thoughts. Just as you might renovate a house to make it more functional and aesthetically pleasing, cognitive restructuring helps you renovate your thought patterns to make them more accurate, helpful, and supportive of your well-being.

Understanding Cognitive Distortions: The Flaws in Our Thinking

At the heart of cognitive restructuring is the idea that our thoughts are not always accurate reflections of reality. Sometimes, our minds play tricks on us, leading us to believe exaggerated, distorted, or untrue things. These thinking errors, known as cognitive distortions, can fuel overthinking, anxiety, and a host of other mental health challenges.

Here are some common cognitive distortions:

- **All-or-Nothing Thinking:** Seeing things in black and white terms, with no shades of gray. For example, believing that you're a complete failure if you don't get a perfect score on a test.

- **Catastrophizing:** Blowing things out of proportion and always expecting the worst-case scenario and thinking that a slight disagreement with your partner will inevitably lead to the end of your relationship.

- **Mental Filtering:** Focusing only on the negative aspects of a situation and ignoring the positive. For example, dwelling on your boss's critical comment and overlooking all the praise you've received.

- **Personalization:** Taking everything personally and blaming yourself for things that are not your fault. For example, believing that your friend's bad mood directly results from something you said or did.

- **Should Statements:** Placing unrealistic expectations on yourself or others, using words like "should," "must," or "ought to." For example, telling yourself, "I should be able to handle this on my own," or "They should have known better."

These cognitive distortions are like mental shortcuts that our brains take to process information quickly. While they might have served an evolutionary purpose in the past, they often lead to inaccurate and unhelpful conclusions in the present day.

The Cognitive Restructuring Process: A Step-by-Step Guide

Cognitive restructuring involves a systematic process of identifying, challenging, and replacing distorted thoughts with more balanced and realistic ones. Here's a simplified version of the process:

1. **Identify the Distorted Thought:** Start by focusing on your thoughts and emotions. When you notice yourself feeling anxious, stressed, or upset, try to pinpoint the Thought that triggered those feelings.

2. **Challenge the Thought:** Ask yourself if the Thought is based on facts or feelings. Look for evidence that supports or contradicts the Thought. Consider alternative explanations for the situation.

3. **Replace the Thought:** Create a more balanced and realistic thought that accurately reflects the situation. This new Thought should be based on evidence and logic rather than fear or negativity.

4. **Practice the New Thought:** Repeat the new Thought to yourself several times, silently and aloud. Write it down, visualize it, or create affirmations based on it. The more you practice the new Thought, the more ingrained it will become in your mind.

Practical Examples and Exercises

Let's walk through a couple of examples of how cognitive restructuring can be applied in real-life situations:

Example 1: Social Anxiety

- **Distorted Thought:** "Everyone at the party will judge me and think I'm boring."

- **Challenge:** "Is there any evidence to support this Thought? Have I been judged harshly at parties in the past? Are there people who enjoy my company?"

- **Replacement Thought:** "I'm interesting and have a lot to offer. Some people will like me, and some won't. That's okay."

Example 2: Work Stress

- **Distorted Thought:** "I'm going to fail this presentation and get fired."

- **Challenge:** "Have I prepared for this presentation? Am I knowledgeable about the topic? Are there people who believe in my abilities?"

- **Replacement Thought:** "I've prepared well for this presentation. I'll do my best; even if it's not perfect, it's not the end of the world."

Cognitive Restructuring Exercises

Here are some exercises you can try to practice cognitive restructuring:

- **Thought Records:** Keep a journal of your negative thoughts, the situations that trigger them, and how you can reframe them.

- **The "What If" Technique:** When you catch yourself catastrophizing, ask yourself, "What if the opposite is true?" or "What's the most likely outcome?"

- **Positive Self-Talk:** Practice using affirmations to counter negative self-talk.

Conclusion: A Calmer, More Rational Mind

By learning to identify and challenge cognitive distortions, you can break free from the cycle of negative thinking and develop a more balanced and realistic outlook on life. Cognitive restructuring is not a quick fix, but with consistent practice, it can be a powerful tool for reducing stress, anxiety, and overthinking. As you rewire your brain for rational thinking, you'll be better equipped to handle life's challenges with grace, confidence, and inner peace.

Self-Reflection Questions:

1. **Negative Thought Patterns:** What are the recurring negative thoughts that often hold you back? Are there any specific themes or situations that trigger these thoughts?

2. **Inner Critic:** How often do you engage in self-criticism? Is your inner critic overly harsh or unrealistic? In what ways does this self-criticism impact your self-esteem and motivation?

3. **Worry vs. Rationality:** When faced with a challenge, do you tend to catastrophize or overthink? How often do you analyze situations rationally and objectively?

4. **Positive Self-Talk:** How often do you engage in positive self-talk? Do you actively challenge negative thoughts with positive affirmations and realistic perspectives?

Transformative Exercises:

1. **Thought Journal:** Keep a daily journal to track your thoughts and emotions. Whenever you notice a negative thought, write it down and then challenge it with a more positive and realistic alternative.

2. **Affirmation Practice:** Create a list of positive affirmations that resonate with you. Repeat these affirmations daily, either out loud or in writing, to reinforce a positive self-image and counteract negative self-talk.

3. **Gratitude Practice:** Cultivate a daily gratitude practice by writing down three things you're grateful for each day. This can help shift your focus towards the positive aspects of your life and counteract negativity.

CHAPTER 6: BUILDING HEALTHY COPING MECHANISMS

"The greatest weapon against stress is our ability to choose one thought over another." - William James

This quote by the renowned psychologist William James speaks volumes about our power to shape our experiences through our thoughts and actions. When it comes to managing stress, anxiety, and overthinking, our lifestyle choices play a pivotal role. By making conscious decisions about how we nourish our bodies, move our bodies, and engage with the world around us, we can build resilience and create a foundation for mental well-being.

Consider this: A study published in the journal "Preventive Medicine" found that individuals who engaged in regular physical activity had a 25% lower risk of developing anxiety disorders compared to those who were inactive. Additionally, research has shown that a healthy diet rich in fruits, vegetables, and whole grains can improve mood and reduce symptoms of depression. These findings highlight the undeniable link between our lifestyle choices and our mental health.

So, how can we harness the power of healthy habits to manage stress, anxiety, and overthinking? Let's explore some key strategies that can transform your life:

1. **Prioritize Sleep:** Sleep is not a luxury; it's necessary for physical and mental health. When we sleep, our bodies repair and restore themselves, and our brains

consolidate memories and process emotions. Aim for 7-8 hours of quality sleep each night. Create a relaxing bedtime routine, avoid caffeine and electronics before bed, and make sure your sleep environment is dark, quiet, and relaxed.

2. **Nourish Your Body:** What you eat directly impacts your mood and energy levels. A diet rich in fruits, vegetables, whole grains, and lean protein can give your brain the nutrients it needs to function optimally. Limit processed foods, sugary drinks, and excessive caffeine, as these can exacerbate anxiety and disrupt sleep.

3. **Move Your Body:** Regular exercise is a powerful antidote to stress and anxiety. When you move, your body releases endorphins, natural mood boosters that can alleviate pain and promote relaxation. Find an activity you enjoy, whether walking, running, swimming, dancing, or yoga. Aim for at least 30 minutes of moderate-intensity exercise most days of the week.

4. **Cultivate Mindfulness:** Mindfulness is the practice of paying attention to the present moment without judgment. It involves observing your thoughts and feelings without getting caught up in them. Mindfulness meditation, deep breathing exercises, and yoga can all help you cultivate a more mindful approach to life, reducing stress and promoting inner peace.

5. **Connect with Others:** Social connection is essential for our well-being. Spending time with loved ones, joining a club or group, or volunteering in your community can provide a sense of belonging and support. Make an effort to connect with others regularly, even if it's just a quick phone call or video chat.

6. **Limit Alcohol and Substance Use:** While it might be tempting to reach for a drink or a drug to relieve stress, these substances can worsen anxiety and depression in the long run. If you're struggling with substance use, seek professional help. There are many resources available to support you on your journey to recovery.

7. **Set Boundaries:** In today's fast-paced world, it's easy to overcommit and become overwhelmed. Learning to say "no" to requests that don't align with your priorities is essential for protecting your time and energy. Set boundaries with work, social obligations, and even your expectations.

8. **Practice Relaxation Techniques:** Many relaxation techniques can help you calm your mind and body. Deep breathing exercises, progressive muscle relaxation, guided imagery, and aromatherapy are just a few examples. Experiment with different techniques to find what works best for you.

9. **Spend Time in Nature:** Numerous studies have shown that spending time in nature can reduce stress, improve

mood, and boost creativity. Take a walk in the park, go for a hike, or sit outside and enjoy the fresh air and sunshine.

Stress-Busting Techniques: Relaxation, Exercise, and Self-Care

Stress is an inevitable part of life. Countless factors can trigger the stress response, from work deadlines to relationship challenges, financial worries, and health concerns. While some stress can motivate, chronic stress can wreak havoc on our physical and mental well-being.

The good news is that you have the power to manage stress and cultivate a calmer, more peaceful state of mind. By incorporating stress-busting techniques into your daily routine, you can build resilience, enhance your well-being, and improve your overall quality of life.

In this section, we'll explore various practical stress-management techniques you can easily integrate into your daily life. Remember, there's no one-size-fits-all approach to stress reduction. Experiment with different techniques and find what works best for you.

Deep Breathing Exercises: Your Portable Stress Reliever

Deep breathing is a simple yet powerful tool for reducing stress and calming the mind. When we're stressed, our breathing tends to become shallow and rapid. This can exacerbate feelings of anxiety and panic. By consciously slowing down and deepening our breath, we can activate the body's relaxation response, lowering heart rate, blood pressure, and muscle tension.

Here's a simple deep breathing exercise you can try:

1. Find a comfortable seated or lying down position.

2. Place one hand on your chest and the other on your abdomen.

3. Inhale slowly through your nose, feeling your abdomen expand as you fill your lungs with air.

4. Hold your breath for a few seconds.

5. Exhale slowly through your mouth, feeling your abdomen contract as you release the air.

6. Repeat for 5-10 minutes.

You can practice this exercise anywhere, anytime you feel stressed or overwhelmed. With regular practice, you'll notice a significant reduction in your overall stress levels.

Progressive Muscle Relaxation: Releasing Tension from Head to Toe

Progressive muscle relaxation (PMR) is a technique that involves systematically tensing and relaxing different muscle groups in your body. This helps you become more aware of physical sensations and teaches you how to release tension.

Here's how to practice PMR:

1. Find a quiet, comfortable place where you won't be disturbed.

2. Close your eyes and take a few deep breaths.

3. Starting with your toes, tense the muscles in your feet as tightly as you can for 5-10 seconds.

4. Release the tension and notice the feeling of relaxation.

5. Move up to your calves, then your thighs, buttocks, stomach, back, chest, shoulders, arms, hands, neck, and face, tensing and relaxing each muscle group in turn.

6. Once you've relaxed all the muscles in your body, take a few more deep breaths and enjoy the feeling of calm.

PMR is a great way to unwind after a stressful day or to prepare for sleep. With regular practice, you'll develop a greater awareness of your body and its tension signals, allowing you to intervene before stress builds up.

Yoga: A Mind-Body Approach to Stress Relief

Yoga is an ancient practice that combines physical postures, breathing exercises, and meditation to promote relaxation and well-being. The gentle stretching and mindful movement of yoga can help release physical tension while focusing on breath, and meditation can calm the mind and reduce stress.

If you're new to yoga, start with a beginner's class or follow a guided online video. Choose a style that suits your fitness level and preferences. Many different types of yoga exist, from gentle restorative yoga to more vigorous vinyasa flows.

Here are some yoga poses that are particularly effective for stress relief:

- **Child's Pose:** This gentle forward fold stretches the back and promotes relaxation.

- **Cat-Cow Pose:** This flowing movement helps release spine and neck tension.

- **Downward-Facing Dog:** This inversion stretches the entire body and can help to calm the mind.

- **Legs-Up-the-Wall Pose:** This restorative pose promotes relaxation and can help to reduce anxiety.

Even a few minutes of yoga each day can make a significant difference in your stress levels. If you don't have time for a full practice, try incorporating a few simple poses into your daily routine. For example, you could do a few stretches in the morning to wake up your body and mind or practice a few calming poses before bed to promote relaxation and sleep.

Spending Time in Nature: The Healing Power of the Great Outdoors

Spending time in nature has a profound impact on our well-being. Research has shown that exposure to nature can reduce stress, anxiety, and depression while boosting mood, creativity, and cognitive function. Whether walking in the park, hiking in the woods, or simply sitting by a lake or ocean, immersing yourself in nature can be a powerful antidote to stress.

Here are some tips for incorporating more nature into your life:

- **Take a daily walk:** Even a short walk in a green space can help to clear your head and reduce stress.

- **Spend time gardening:** Getting your hands dirty in the soil can be a therapeutic and grounding experience.

- **Plan outdoor activities:** Go for a hike, bike ride, or kayaking trip. Spend a weekend camping or exploring a new park.

- **Bring nature indoors:** Decorate your home with plants, flowers, and natural materials.

Engaging in Hobbies: The Joy of Doing What You Love

Engaging in hobbies and activities, you enjoy can be a powerful way to relieve stress and boost your mood. When you're engrossed in a hobby, you enter a state of flow where you're fully immersed in the present moment, and your worries fade away.

Whether painting, playing music, dancing, cooking, reading, writing, or simply spending time with loved ones, make time for activities that bring you joy and fulfillment. Hobbies provide a much-needed break from the stresses of daily life and allow you to recharge your batteries.

Here are some tips for incorporating hobbies into your stress-management routine:

- **Schedule time for your hobbies:** Set aside specific times for your hobbies, just as you would for work or other commitments. This will help ensure that you make time for activities that nourish your soul.

- **Try something new:** Feel free to experiment with different hobbies and activities. You might be surprised at what you enjoy.

- **Join a club or group:** Connecting with others who share your interests can be a great way to make new friends, learn new skills, and find support.

- **Don't put pressure on yourself:** The goal of a hobby is to have fun and relax. Don't worry about being perfect or achieving any particular outcome. Just enjoy the process of creating, learning, or simply being.

Additional Stress-Busting Techniques

In addition to the techniques mentioned above, here are a few other stress-busters you might find helpful:

- **Mindful Eating:** Pay attention to your food's taste, texture, and smell. This can help you slow down, savor your meals, and reduce stress.

- **Aromatherapy:** Certain scents, like lavender, chamomile, and sandalwood, can be calming. Use essential oils in a diffuser, or add a few drops to your bath.

- **Massage Therapy:** Massage can help to release muscle tension, improve circulation, and reduce stress hormones.

- **Music Therapy:** Listening to calming music or nature sounds can help to soothe the mind and body.

- **Spending Time with Pets:** Interacting with animals has been shown to reduce stress, anxiety, and blood pressure.

Remember, the key to effective stress management is to find what works for you. Experiment with different techniques and create a personalized toolkit to turn to whenever you feel stressed or overwhelmed. By making stress-busting a regular part of your routine, you can cultivate a calmer, more resilient, and more joyful life.

Healthy Habits for a Calm Mind: Sleep, Nutrition, and Social Connection

Think of your body and mind as a finely tuned instrument. Just as a musical instrument needs regular care and maintenance to produce beautiful music, your body and mind require nourishment and attention to function optimally.

Overthinking, stress, and anxiety can disrupt this delicate balance, throwing your whole system out of tune. However, by adopting healthy habits, you can restore harmony and cultivate a calmer, more resilient mind.

Let's explore four essential well-being pillars crucial for managing overthinking and promoting mental health: sleep, nutrition, exercise, and social connection. By prioritizing these areas, you'll reduce stress and anxiety and enhance your overall quality of life.

The Importance of Sleep: Recharging Your Mental Battery

Sleep is not merely a time for rest; it's a period of essential rejuvenation for your body and mind. During sleep, your brain processes information, consolidates memories, and repairs itself. Your cognitive function, mood, and emotional regulation suffer when you don't get enough sleep.

Overthinkers often struggle with sleep, as their minds continue to race even when their bodies crave rest. Chronic sleep deprivation can exacerbate anxiety, depression, and other mental health problems, making it even harder to break free from the cycle of overthinking.

Here are some tips for improving your sleep hygiene:

- **Establish a consistent sleep schedule:** Go to bed and wake up at the same time each day, even on weekends. This helps to regulate your body's natural sleep-wake cycle.

- **Create a relaxing bedtime routine:** Avoid screens for at least an hour before bed. Instead, read a book, take a warm bath, or listen to calming music.

- **Make your bedroom conducive to sleep:** Keep your bedroom calm, dark, and quiet. Invest in a comfortable mattress and pillows.

- **Limit caffeine and alcohol:** Avoid caffeine and alcohol in the hours leading up to bedtime, as they can interfere with sleep.

- **Seek help if you have chronic sleep problems:** If you consistently struggle with insomnia or other sleep disorders, consult a doctor or sleep specialist.

Nutrition: Fueling Your Brain and Body for Optimal Function

The food you eat directly impacts your mood, energy levels, and cognitive function. A healthy diet can help to reduce stress, anxiety, and inflammation while promoting a calmer, more focused mind.

Overthinkers often turn to unhealthy comfort foods in times of stress, but these foods can exacerbate their symptoms. Processed foods, sugary drinks, and excessive caffeine can lead to blood sugar spikes and crashes, mood swings, and difficulty concentrating.

Here are some tips for eating a balanced diet that supports mental well-being:

- **Eat plenty of fruits and vegetables:** These nutrients provide essential vitamins, minerals, and antioxidants that protect your brain and body from stress.

- **Choose whole grains over refined grains:** Whole grains provide sustained energy and fiber, which can help regulate blood sugar levels and mood.

- **Incorporate healthy fats:** Omega-3 fatty acids in fatty fish, nuts, and seeds are essential for brain health and can help reduce anxiety and depression.

- **Limit processed foods, sugary drinks, and caffeine:** These substances can disrupt your blood sugar levels, mood, and sleep.

- **Stay hydrated:** Drink plenty of water throughout the day to support brain function and overall health.

Exercise: Your Natural Mood Booster

Exercise is not just about physical fitness; it's a powerful tool for managing stress and improving mental health. Regular physical activity has been shown to reduce anxiety, depression, and negative mood while boosting self-esteem and cognitive function.

Overthinkers often neglect exercise, as they may feel too overwhelmed or exhausted to get moving. However, even moderate exercise can make a significant difference. Exercise releases endorphins, natural chemicals in the brain that have mood-boosting and pain-relieving effects.

Here are some tips for establishing an exercise routine:

- **Find an activity you enjoy:** Walking, running, swimming, dancing, or playing a sport; choose an activity that you find fun and rewarding.

- **Start slowly and gradually increase intensity:** If you're new to exercise, start with short, low-intensity workouts and gradually increase the duration and intensity over time.

- **Set realistic goals:** Don't try to do too much too soon. Set achievable goals that you can build upon over time.

- **Find a workout buddy:** Exercising with a friend or family member can help you stay motivated and accountable.

- **Make exercise a part of your routine:** Schedule time for exercise in your daily or weekly schedule and treat it like any other important appointment.

Social Connection: The Importance of Human Bonds

Humans are social creatures and meaningful connections with others are essential to our well-being. Social isolation and loneliness can increase stress, anxiety, and depression, while strong social bonds can provide a buffer against these negative emotions.

Overthinkers often withdraw from social interactions, as they may feel self-conscious, insecure, or overwhelmed by social situations. However, isolating yourself can worsen overthinking and anxiety.

Here are some tips for fostering meaningful relationships:

- **Make time for loved ones:** Prioritize spending time with family and friends who make you feel supported and understood.

- **Join a club or group:** Find a group of people who share your interests, whether it's a book club, sports team, or volunteer organization.

- **Volunteer your time:** Helping others can give you a sense of purpose and connection to your community.

- **Reach out to a therapist or counselor:** If you're struggling with social anxiety or isolation, a therapist can help you develop coping skills and build stronger relationships.

By prioritizing sleep, nutrition, exercise, and social connection, you can create a solid foundation for mental well-being and resilience. These healthy habits can help you manage overthinking, reduce stress and anxiety, and cultivate a calmer, more joyful life.

Self-Reflection Questions:

1. **Stress Inventory:** What are your primary sources of stress? Are they work-related, relationship-related, or something else? How does stress typically manifest in your body and mind (e.g., muscle tension, racing thoughts, irritability)?

2. **Current Coping Strategies:** How do you currently cope with stress? Are your methods healthy and sustainable, or do they involve unhealthy habits like excessive caffeine, alcohol, or emotional eating?

3. **Self-Care Routine:** Do you have a regular self-care routine? If so, what does it consist of? If not, what

activities would you like to incorporate to prioritize your well-being?

4. **Sleep Habits:** How would you rate the quality and quantity of your sleep? Do you often feel rested and energized upon waking, or do you struggle with fatigue and difficulty concentrating?

Transformative Exercises:

1. **Relaxation Techniques:** Experiment with various relaxation techniques like deep breathing exercises, progressive muscle relaxation, or guided imagery. Find one or two that resonate with you and incorporate them into your daily routine.

2. **Mindful Movement:** Engage in regular physical activity that you enjoy, whether it's walking, running, dancing, or yoga. Exercise can be a powerful stress reliever and mood booster.

3. **Self-Care Rituals:** Create a personalized self-care ritual that incorporates activities that nurture your mind, body, and spirit. This could include taking a warm bath, reading a book, listening to calming music, or spending time in nature.

4. **Sleep Hygiene Optimization:** Establish a consistent sleep schedule, create a relaxing bedtime routine, and ensure your sleep environment is conducive to rest. Avoid caffeine and electronics in the hours before bed.

5. **Social Connection Challenge:** Make an effort to connect with someone every day, whether it's a friend, family member, or colleague. Engage in meaningful conversations, offer support, and ask for help when you need it.

CHAPTER 7: LIVING IN THE MOMENT

"The present moment is filled with joy and happiness. If you are attentive, you will see it." Thich Nhat Hanh, a Vietnamese Buddhist monk, beautifully captured the essence of mindfulness and the transformative power of living in the present moment. In today's fast-paced world, our minds often race from one thought to the next, dwelling on the past or worrying about the future. We get caught in a whirlwind of anxieties, regrets, and "what ifs," leaving little room for appreciating the here and now.

But what if there was a way to break free from this mental chaos? What if we could find a sense of peace and contentment amidst the busyness of life? That's where mindfulness comes in. Mindfulness is the practice of paying full attention to the present moment without judgment. It's about being aware of our thoughts, emotions, and bodily sensations as they arise without getting caught up in them.

Think of it like this: imagine your mind is a river. Your thoughts and emotions are like leaves floating on the surface. When you're not mindful, you get swept away by the current, clinging to the leaves and tangled in their stories. But when you practice mindfulness, you stand on the riverbank, observing the leaves as they pass by. You acknowledge them, but you don't let them control you.

This simple shift in perspective can have a profound impact on our well-being. Research has shown that mindfulness can reduce stress, anxiety, and depression while improving focus, creativity, and emotional regulation. It can also help us break free from the cycle of overthinking as we learn to observe our thoughts without getting caught up in them.

So, how do we cultivate mindfulness in our daily lives? It starts with paying attention to the small details of our experiences. Notice the feeling of the sun on your skin, the taste of your morning coffee, and the sound of the birds singing. When you're eating, focus on the flavors and textures of your food. When walking, pay attention to the sensation of your feet hitting the ground.

Mindfulness isn't just about paying attention to the external world, it's also about tuning in to our internal experiences. Notice your emotions as they arise, without judging them or trying to change them. Simply observe them with curiosity and acceptance.

When your mind starts to wander – and it will – gently bring your attention back to the present moment. Don't get discouraged if your mind wanders frequently. It's a natural part of the process. The key is to keep practicing; eventually, you'll find that you can stay focused for longer periods.

One of the most powerful benefits of mindfulness is its ability to help us break free from the tyranny of overthinking. When we're mindful, we learn to observe our thoughts without getting caught up in them. We can recognize that our thoughts are just thoughts, not facts. This realization can be incredibly liberating, as it allows us to step back from our worries and anxieties and see them in a new light.

Mindfulness also helps us to cultivate a greater appreciation for the present moment. We can fully engage with the here and now when we're not constantly dwelling on the past or worrying about the future. This allows us to experience more joy, gratitude, and connection with the world around us.

Imagine going for a walk in the park. When you're not mindful, you might be so caught up in your thoughts that you barely notice the trees, the flowers, or the birdsong. But when you're mindful, you can fully appreciate nature's beauty, the sun's warmth on your skin, and the sound of leaves rustling in the wind. You might even notice the subtle details of a flower petal or the intricate patterns of a spider web.

Learning to live in the moment allows us to tap into a deeper sense of peace and contentment. We can find joy in the simple things, appreciate the people in our lives, and feel more connected to the world.

Living in the moment doesn't mean ignoring our problems or pretending everything is perfect. It means focusing on what is happening right now rather than getting lost in the past or worrying about the future. When we can do this, we open ourselves up to the possibility of experiencing life more fully, with greater clarity, joy, and gratitude.

Embrace the Present: The Power of Now

It's easy to get caught up in the whirlwind of thoughts and worries. We often find ourselves dwelling on the past or anxiously anticipating the future, completely missing out on the present moment. But what if I told you that the key to a calmer, more fulfilling life lies in embracing the here and now?

This is where mindfulness comes in. Mindfulness is the practice of paying full attention to the present moment without judgment. It's about being aware of your thoughts, feelings, bodily sensations, and the world around you, without getting caught up in them.

Think of your mind as a monkey swinging from one thought to the next. Mindfulness is like gently placing that monkey back on your shoulder, allowing you to observe your thoughts without getting carried away. It's about being present with whatever arises in your experience, whether pleasant or unpleasant, without trying to change it or push it away.

The Benefits of Mindfulness: A More Peaceful and Joyful Life

Mindfulness is not just a trendy buzzword; it's a practice with profound benefits for your mental, emotional, and physical well-being.

Research has shown that mindfulness can:

- **Reduce Stress and Anxiety:** By focusing on the present moment, you can quiet the mental chatter that fuels stress and anxiety. Mindfulness helps you become more aware of your thoughts and emotions, allowing you to respond to them more skillfully rather than getting swept away.

- **Improve Focus and Concentration:** When you're mindful, you're less likely to get distracted by your thoughts or external stimuli. This can lead to improved focus and concentration at work and in your personal life.

- **Enhance Emotional Regulation:** Mindfulness helps you become more aware of your emotions and their triggers. This awareness allows you to choose how you respond to your feelings rather than reacting impulsively.

- **Boost Self-Awareness:** By paying attention to your thoughts, feelings, and bodily sensations, you develop a deeper understanding of yourself and your behavior patterns. This self-awareness can help you make more conscious choices and live a more authentic life.

- **Improve Relationships:** When you're fully present with others, you listen more deeply, communicate more effectively, and build stronger connections. Mindfulness can help cultivate empathy, compassion, and understanding in your relationships.

- **Increase Resilience:** By learning to accept and embrace all of your positive and negative experiences, you become more resilient in the face of challenges. Mindfulness can help you to bounce back from setbacks more quickly and to find meaning and growth in difficult situations.

Mindfulness in Everyday Life: Practical Techniques

Mindfulness is not something that you only practice during formal meditation sessions. It's a way of being that you can cultivate throughout your day, no matter what you're doing. Here are a few simple techniques for bringing mindfulness into your everyday activities:

- **Mindful Eating:** Instead of mindlessly scarfing down your food while scrolling through your phone, try eating with full attention. Notice the colors, textures, and aromas of your food. Savor each bite, paying attention to the flavors and sensations in your mouth.

- **Mindful Walking:** As you walk, pay attention to the sensation of your feet hitting the ground. Notice the rhythm of your breath and the feeling of the air on your skin. Take in the sights and sounds around you as if you're seeing them for the first time.

- **Mindful Chores:** Even mundane tasks like washing dishes or folding laundry can be opportunities for mindfulness. Instead of rushing through them, focus on the sensations of your hands moving, the warmth of the water, or the smell of the detergent.

- **Mindful Breathing:** Take a few moments to pause and focus on your breath throughout your day. Notice the rise and fall of your chest or abdomen. Feel the air entering and leaving your nostrils. This simple practice can anchor you in the present moment and reduce stress.

- **Mindful Listening:** When talking to someone, give them your full attention. Put away your phone, make eye contact, and listen to what they're saying without interrupting or formulating your response.

- **Mindful Driving:** Instead of getting caught up in road rage or zoning out, pay attention to the sensations of driving. Notice the feeling of the steering wheel in your hands, the pressure of your foot on the gas pedal, and the sounds of the engine and the road.

The key to cultivating mindfulness is to practice regularly, even if it's just for a few minutes each day. The more you practice, the more natural it will become and the more benefits you'll experience.

Gratitude and Joy: Finding Sunshine in the Rain

We often overlook the simple joys and blessings surrounding us, focusing instead on what we lack or what's going wrong.

But what if there was a way to shift our focus from negativity to positivity, to cultivate a sense of contentment and well-being even amidst life's challenges?

The answer lies in the power of gratitude and joy.

Gratitude: The Antidote to Negativity

Gratitude is acknowledging and appreciating the good things in our lives. It's about recognizing the kindness of others, the beauty of nature, the simple pleasures of everyday life, and the countless blessings that we often take for granted.

When we cultivate gratitude, we shift our focus from what we lack to what we have. We become more aware of the positive aspects of our lives, and our minds become less consumed by worry, regret, and dissatisfaction.

Research has shown that gratitude has a profound impact on our well-being. It can:

- **Reduce stress and anxiety:** When we focus on the good things in our lives, we activate the parasympathetic nervous system, which is responsible for rest and relaxation. This can help to lower our heart rate, blood pressure, and stress hormone levels.

- **Improve sleep:** Gratitude has been shown to improve sleep quality and duration. When we go to bed with a grateful heart, we're less likely to be kept awake by worries and ruminations.

- **Boost mood and happiness:** Gratitude can increase the production of dopamine and serotonin, neurotransmitters that are associated with pleasure and happiness.

- **Strengthen relationships:** Expressing gratitude to others can deepen our connections with them and create a positive feedback loop of appreciation and kindness.

- **Increase resilience:** Grateful people tend to be more resilient in the face of adversity. They're able to find meaning and purpose even in difficult situations, and they're more likely to bounce back from setbacks.

Practicing Gratitude: Simple Exercises for a Happier You

Cultivating gratitude doesn't have to be complicated. In fact, some of the most effective gratitude practices are simple and can be easily incorporated into your daily routine.

Here are a few exercises to get you started:

1. **Gratitude Journaling:** Take a few minutes each day to write down three things you're grateful for. These can be big or small, from the roof over your head to a delicious cup of coffee. The key is to focus on your life's positive aspects and savor the feelings of appreciation.

2. **Gratitude Jar:** Find a jar or container and decorate it however you like. Write down something you're grateful for each day on a slip of paper and place it in the jar. At the end of the week, month, or year, read through the slips of paper and reflect on all the good things that have happened in your life.

3. **Gratitude Letters:** Write a letter or text to someone who has positively impacted your life. Express your appreciation for their kindness, support, or guidance. You can choose to send the letter or keep it for yourself.

4. **Gratitude Meditation:** Sit quietly and focus on your breath for a few minutes. As you inhale, think of something you're grateful for. As you exhale, release any tension or negativity. Repeat for several minutes.

5. **Expressing Gratitude to Others:** Make a conscious effort to thank people for their kindness, whether it's a

friend who listened to you vent, a stranger who held the door open, or a colleague who helped you with a project. A simple "thank you" can go a long way in brightening someone's day and strengthening your connection with them.

Remember, gratitude is a muscle that needs to be exercised regularly. The more you practice gratitude, the more naturally it will become a part of your life.

Finding Joy in the Simple Things: The Key to Everyday Happiness

While gratitude is about appreciating the good things in our lives, joy is finding pleasure and delight in the present moment. It's about savoring the taste of your morning coffee, feeling the warmth of the sun on your skin, laughing with a friend, or simply enjoying the quiet stillness of a peaceful evening.

Joy is not about chasing after fleeting pleasures or material possessions. It's about finding contentment in the everyday moments of our lives. When we're able to find joy in the simple things, we become less reliant on external sources of happiness and more resilient in the face of life's challenges.

Self-Reflection Questions:

1. **Present Moment Awareness:** How often do you find yourself dwelling on the past or worrying about the future? When was the last time you felt truly present in the moment, fully engaged with what you were doing?

2. **Gratitude Reflection:** What are three things you are grateful for right now? How does focusing on gratitude shift your perspective and mood?

3. **Joyful Moments:** What activities or experiences bring you the most joy? How often do you prioritize these activities in your daily life?

4. **Mind Wandering:** When your mind wanders, where does it usually go? Is it drawn to regrets, anxieties, or pleasant memories? Understanding your mind's tendencies can help you redirect it toward the present.

5. **Positive Focus:** Do you tend to focus more on problems or possibilities? How can you shift your focus to the positive aspects of your life, even in challenging situations?

Transformative Exercises:

1. **Mindfulness Meditation:** Practice mindfulness meditation for 5-10 minutes each day, focusing on your breath, bodily sensations, or sounds in your environment. This helps cultivate present moment awareness and reduce mind wandering.

2. **Gratitude Journaling:** Write down three things you are grateful for each day. This simple practice can significantly increase your overall sense of well-being and happiness.

3. **Joyful Activities Calendar:** Create a calendar specifically for scheduling activities that bring you joy.

Make a conscious effort to incorporate these activities into your weekly routine.

4. **Mindful Observation:** Choose a simple activity like eating, walking, or washing dishes. Engage all your senses as you perform the activity, noticing the sights, sounds, smells, tastes, and textures. This can help anchor you in the present moment and cultivate appreciation for everyday experiences.

5. **Positive Affirmations:** Start each day by repeating positive affirmations that focus on your strengths, capabilities, and gratitude. This sets a positive tone for the day and helps you maintain a more optimistic outlook.

CHAPTER 8: YOUR PATH TO FREEDOM

"The greatest weapon against stress is our ability to choose one thought over another." - William James.

Overthinking is a common struggle affecting millions of people worldwide. It's a relentless mental habit that can steal our joy, drain our energy, and hinder our ability to live fully in the present moment. But here's the empowering truth: you are not powerless against overthinking. You can break free from its grip and reclaim your mental peace.

Throughout this book, we've explored the intricate workings of the overthinking mind, its connection to stress and anxiety, and the numerous strategies you can employ to manage and overcome it. Now, it's time to take all that you've learned and create a personalized plan for your journey to freedom.

Think of this chapter as your personal roadmap, guiding you toward a life beyond overthinking. It's not about following a rigid set of rules but about discovering what works best for you and tailoring your approach to your unique needs and preferences.

This journey begins with self-reflection. Take a moment to review the various techniques and strategies we've discussed. Which ones resonated most with you? Which ones felt like they could truly make a difference in your life? Identify the tools you're most drawn to that fit seamlessly into your daily routine.

Perhaps you found solace in the simplicity of deep breathing exercises, or maybe the mindfulness practice resonated with your desire for greater present-moment awareness. You might have discovered that journaling helps you declutter your mind or that spending time in nature provides a much-needed respite from anxious thoughts.

Whatever tools you choose, remember that consistency is key. Just as a musician practices their instrument daily to improve their skills, you need to practice these stress-busting techniques regularly to reap their benefits. Make them a non-negotiable part of your routine, just like brushing your teeth or eating breakfast.

As you embark on this journey, be patient with yourself. Changing ingrained thought patterns and habits takes time and effort. There will be days when overthinking seems to take over, and that's okay. Don't beat yourself up or give up on your goals. Instead, view these moments as opportunities for growth and learning.

Remember, you're not alone in this struggle. Millions of people have overcome overthinking and live happier, healthier, and more fulfilling lives. With the right tools, support, and determination, you can too.

So, take a deep breath, release any lingering doubts or fears, and step confidently onto your path to freedom. This is your journey, and you have the power to make it a successful one.

Your Personalized Toolkit: Crafting a Stress-Relief Strategy That Works for You

Throughout this book, we've explored a wide array of strategies for managing overthinking and stress. From understanding the overthinking mind to reframing negative thoughts, cultivating mindfulness to building healthy coping mechanisms, you now have a toolbox filled with powerful tools to reclaim your mental peace.

But here's the key: There's no one-size-fits-all solution. What works wonders for one person may not be as effective for another. That's why creating a personalized toolkit, a stress-relief strategy tailored to your unique needs, preferences, and lifestyle is crucial.

Think of it like building your custom playlist for stress relief. Just as you choose songs that resonate with your mood and taste, you'll select the stress-busting techniques that feel most natural and enjoyable to you. By incorporating these practices into your daily or weekly routine, you'll create a sustainable and effective way to manage overthinking and cultivate a calmer, more resilient mind.

Step 1: Take Inventory of Your Stressors

Before you can build your toolkit, it's essential to understand what triggers your overthinking and stress. What situations, thoughts, or events tend to send your mind into overdrive? Are there specific times of day or week when you're more prone to worry?

Take some time to reflect on your typical stressors. You might find it helpful to keep a journal for a few days and jot down the moments when you feel most stressed or anxious. By identifying your triggers, you can tailor your stress-management strategies accordingly.

Step 2: Identify Your Go-To Stress-Relief Techniques

Now that you know what triggers your stress, it's time to identify the techniques that work best for you. Think back to the strategies we've discussed in this book. Which ones resonated with you the most? Which ones did you find most enjoyable or effective?

Consider the following:

- **Deep Breathing:** Did you find that taking a few deep breaths helped to calm you down and clear your head?

- **Progressive Muscle Relaxation:** Did you feel a sense of release and relaxation after practicing PMR?

- **Yoga:** Did you enjoy the combination of physical movement and mindfulness that yoga offers?

- **Spending Time in Nature:** Did you feel more grounded and peaceful after a walk in the park or a hike in the woods?

- **Engaging in Hobbies:** Did you find that losing yourself in a favorite activity helped to distract you from your worries and boost your mood?

- **Positive Self-Talk:** Did replacing negative thoughts with positive affirmations help to shift your mindset and reduce anxiety?

- **Mindfulness and Meditation:** Did practicing mindfulness help you to become more aware of your thoughts and emotions and to respond to them with greater clarity and compassion?

- **Other Techniques:** Did any other stress-management techniques, such as mindful eating, aromatherapy, massage therapy, or spending time with pets, resonate with you?

There's no right or wrong answer here. The most effective stress-relief techniques are the ones that you enjoy and that fit seamlessly into your lifestyle.

Step 3: Create a Personalized Stress-Management Plan

Once you've identified your go-to techniques, it's time to create a personalized stress-management plan. This plan should include a combination of daily and weekly practices that you can easily incorporate into your routine.

Here are some examples of how you might structure your plan:

- **Daily Practices:**

  - Start your day with a few minutes of deep breathing or mindfulness meditation.

  - Incorporate a short yoga or stretching routine into your morning or evening.

- Take a 10-minute walk in nature during your lunch break.

- Practice positive self-talk throughout the day, especially when you notice negative thoughts creeping in.

- End your day with relaxing activities such as reading, listening to calming music, or taking a warm bath.

- **Weekly Practices:**

  - Schedule a longer yoga class or outdoor activity, such as hiking or kayaking.

  - Dedicate time to a favorite hobby, such as painting, playing music, or spending time with friends.

  - Get a massage or try aromatherapy to promote relaxation.

  - Reflect on your week and identify any patterns of stress or overthinking.

Your plan should be flexible and adaptable. If a specific technique isn't working for you, don't be afraid to try something else. The most important thing is to find practices you enjoy that help you feel calmer and more centered.

Step 4: Track Your Progress and Adjust as Needed

As you implement your stress-management plan, take some time to track your progress. How are you feeling? Are you noticing changes in your stress levels, sleep patterns, or overall well-being?

Don't get discouraged if you find that your plan isn't working as well as you'd like. Make some adjustments and try again. Remember, managing stress is an ongoing process. It's about finding what works for you and making it a sustainable part of your life.

By creating a personalized toolkit, you're empowering yourself to take control of your stress and overthinking. With consistent practice and a willingness to experiment, you can cultivate a calmer, more resilient, and more joyful life.

Celebrate Your Successes: The Power of Acknowledging Progress

The journey to overcome overthinking is not a sprint; it's a marathon. It's a path filled with ups and downs, twists and turns. There will be days when you feel like you're making great strides and other days when you stumble and fall back into old patterns.

It's important to remember that progress is not always linear. There will be setbacks along the way, but that doesn't mean you're failing. Setbacks can be valuable learning experiences that help you grow and become stronger.

One of the most important things you can do on this journey is to celebrate your successes, no matter how small they may seem.

Why Celebrating Success Matters

Celebrating your successes is not about vanity or bragging. It's about acknowledging your hard work, recognizing your progress, and reinforcing positive behaviors. When you take the time to celebrate your wins, you're sending a powerful message to your brain: "This is important. This is worth doing." This positive reinforcement can motivate you to keep going, even when faced with challenges.

Celebrating your successes can also help to:

- **Boost your confidence:** When you acknowledge your accomplishments, you build self-efficacy, the belief in your ability to succeed.

- **Increase your motivation:** Celebrating your wins can give you the energy and enthusiasm to tackle new challenges.

- **Reduce stress and anxiety:** Focusing on the positive can help to shift your mindset away from worry and self-doubt.

- **Improve your overall well-being:** When you feel good about yourself and your progress, it can enhance your mood, relationships, and overall quality of life.

How to Celebrate Your Successes

There's no right or wrong way to celebrate your successes. The most important thing is finding what feels meaningful and authentic. Here are a few ideas to get you started:

- **Treat Yourself:** Indulge in a small reward, such as a favorite food, a relaxing bath, or a new book.

- **Share Your Success:** Tell a friend, family member, or therapist about your accomplishment. Sharing your joy with others can amplify it.

- **Write it Down:** Keep a journal of your big and small successes. This can be a source of inspiration and encouragement when you're feeling discouraged.

- **Reflect on Your Progress:** Take some time to think about how far you've come. What have you learned? What challenges have you overcome?

- **Set New Goals:** Use your success as motivation to set new goals and continue your growth journey.

Examples of Small Victories to Celebrate

Remember, progress doesn't always have to be monumental. Here are some examples of small victories that are worth celebrating on your journey to overcome overthinking:

- **Catching a Negative Thought:** The first step to changing negative self-talk is awareness. If you see yourself engaging in negative thinking and can reframe it, that's a win!

- **Practicing a Stress-Management Technique:** Whether taking a few deep breaths, going for a walk, or meditating for five minutes, any effort you make to manage your stress is a victory.

- **Saying No to Something That Doesn't Serve You:** Learning to set boundaries and prioritize your needs is important in reducing overthinking and anxiety.

- **Asking for Help:** Reaching out for support, whether from a friend, family member, or therapist, is a sign of strength, not weakness.

- **Taking a Break from Overthinking:** If you can step away from a worry cycle, even for a few minutes, that's a significant accomplishment.

- **Noticing a Positive Change:** Perhaps you're sleeping better, feeling more relaxed, or experiencing less anxiety. These are all signs that you're making progress.

Overcoming Setbacks: Learning from Your Mistakes

As mentioned earlier, setbacks are a natural part of any journey of growth and change. Don't let them discourage you or derail your progress. Instead, view them as opportunities for learning and self-reflection.

Here are some tips for overcoming setbacks:

- **Acknowledge Your Feelings:** Feeling frustrated, disappointed, or discouraged when you experience a setback is okay. Allow yourself to feel these emotions without judgment.

- **Identify the Cause:** Try to understand what led to the setback. Did you encounter a trigger? Did you slip back into old habits? Once you know the cause, you can take steps to prevent it from happening again.

- **Learn from Your Mistakes:** View the setback as a learning experience. What can you do differently next time? How can you use this experience to grow?

- **Practice Self-Compassion:** Be kind to yourself. Everyone makes mistakes, and setbacks are a normal part of the learning process.

- **Reach Out for Support:** Talk to a friend, family member, or therapist if you feel overwhelmed or discouraged.

Self-Reflection Questions:

1. **Personalized Toolkit Review:** Reflecting on the strategies and techniques discussed in this book, which ones resonated most with you? Which ones do you feel would be most effective in your own journey to overcome overthinking?

2. **Plan Implementation:** How can you incorporate these chosen strategies into your daily life? What specific actions can you take, and what obstacles might you encounter along the way? How can you prepare for these obstacles?

3. **Success Recognition:** Take a moment to acknowledge the progress you've made so far. What small victories have you achieved in managing your overthinking tendencies? How have these wins positively impacted your life?

4. **Gratitude Practice:** What are you grateful for in your life right now? How can cultivating gratitude help you shift your focus away from overthinking and towards appreciating the present moment?

5. **Life Beyond Overthinking:** Imagine a life where overthinking no longer holds you back. What would that life look like? What goals would you pursue? How would you feel? Visualizing this future can be a powerful motivator for change.

Transformative Exercises:

1. **Create Your Toolkit:** Design a personalized toolkit for managing overthinking. Include your chosen strategies, techniques, and reminders that resonate with you. Keep this toolkit accessible so you can refer to it whenever you need support.

2. **Daily Action Plan:** Develop a daily action plan that incorporates at least one strategy from your toolkit. Start small and gradually increase the frequency and intensity of your practice.

3. **Success Journal:** Start a success journal to document your achievements, both big and small. Record your

progress, your feelings, and any lessons learned along the way.

4. **Gratitude Jar:** Write down things you're grateful for on small slips of paper and place them in a jar. Whenever you feel overwhelmed by overthinking, pull out a slip and read it aloud.

5. **Vision Board or Collage:** Create a visual representation of your life beyond overthinking. Gather images, quotes, and objects that represent your goals, dreams, and aspirations. Display this vision board where you'll see it daily to reinforce your commitment to change.

EMBRACING A LIFE BEYOND OVERTHINKING

"The mind is a superb instrument if used rightly. Used wrongly, however, it becomes very destructive." — Eckhart Tolle

Overthinking, while a common human experience, doesn't have to dictate your life. It can be a relentless thief, stealing your joy, peace, and well-being. But armed with the knowledge and tools we've explored in this book, you have the power to break free from its grasp and reclaim your mental freedom.

Throughout these chapters, we've journeyed together through the labyrinthine corridors of the overthinking mind. We've uncovered the intricate connection between overthinking and stress, explored its devastating impact on our health, relationships, and happiness, and, most importantly, discovered a wealth of practical strategies for taming this unruly beast.

Let's recap the key takeaways from our journey:

- **Understanding the Overthinking Mind:** We've learned that overthinking is a habit, not a personality trait. It's a cycle of repetitive thoughts fueled by anxiety and fear. But by understanding its roots and recognizing the patterns, we can begin to dismantle it.

- **The Stress Connection:** We've seen how overthinking triggers the stress response, flooding our bodies with cortisol and other stress hormones. This chronic stress can wreak havoc on our physical and mental health, but by managing stress, we can break the cycle of overthinking.

- **Taming Anxiety:** We've explored the link between overthinking and anxiety and learned how to recognize and manage anxiety symptoms. By cultivating a calmer mind, we can reduce the intensity and frequency of anxious thoughts.

- **Decluttering the Mind:** We've discovered the power of mindfulness, meditation, and journaling to quiet the mental chatter and create space for peace and clarity. We can gain perspective and make better decisions by clearing the mental clutter.

- **Reframing Negative Thoughts:** We've learned how to challenge and reframe negative self-talk, replacing self-criticism with self-compassion and doubt with confidence. We can rewrite our narratives and create a more empowering outlook by cultivating a positive inner dialogue.

- **Building Healthy Coping Mechanisms:** We've explored many stress-busting techniques, from deep breathing and yoga to spending time in nature and pursuing hobbies. By incorporating these practices into our daily lives, we can build resilience and manage stress more effectively.

- **Living in the Moment:** We've learned the importance of embracing the present moment and cultivating gratitude for the simple joys of life. By focusing on the here and now, we can break free from the cycle of rumination and worry.

Your Path to Freedom: A Continuous Journey

As you embark on your journey to overcome overthinking, remember that it's not about eliminating all thoughts or striving for a perfectly quiet mind. Instead, it's about learning to manage your thoughts, emotions, and reactions in a healthier way. It's about finding a balance between reflection and action, worry and trust, and past regrets and future anxieties.

Your path to freedom is unique and will require ongoing effort and self-compassion. There will be setbacks and challenges, but don't let them discourage you. Every small step you take towards a calmer mind is a victory worth celebrating.

Embrace the Journey with Hope and Determination

Remember, you are not alone in this struggle. Millions of people grapple with overthinking, and many have found their way to a more peaceful and fulfilling life. With the tools and strategies you've learned in this book, you too can break free from the chains of overthinking and embrace a brighter future.

Imagine a life where your mind is your ally, not your enemy. A life where you can confidently make decisions, approach challenges with resilience, and savor the present moment without fear or regret—a life where you can truly thrive, not just survive.

This life is within your reach. It starts with a commitment to yourself, a willingness to learn and grow, and a belief that you can change.

The road ahead may not always be easy, but it will be worth it. So take a deep breath, let go of the worries that weigh you down, and step into the unknown with courage and hope.

A brighter future awaits you. Your journey begins now..

A Heartfelt Note to My Readers

Dear Reader,

As I write these words, excitement, gratitude, and a touch of nervous anticipation wash over me. This book, **"Beyond Overthinking: A Step-by-Step Approach to Declutter Your Mind, Relieve Stress, Manage Anxiety, and Live in the Moment,"** has been a labor of love, a journey of self-discovery, and a testament to the power of the human spirit to overcome challenges.

I poured my heart and soul into these pages, drawing from personal experiences, research, and the wisdom of countless individuals who have navigated the treacherous waters of overthinking. This book will serve as a beacon of light, guiding you toward a calmer mind, a more peaceful heart, and a life filled with joy and purpose.

If you're reading this, it means you've taken the courageous step of seeking help for your overthinking. Perhaps you've been struggling with anxiety, stress, or a relentless inner critic that won't let you rest. Maybe you've felt trapped in a cycle of worry and self-doubt, longing for a way out.

I want you to know that you're not alone. Overthinking is a common struggle, but it doesn't have to define you. This book is your roadmap to freedom, offering practical tools and strategies to break free from the grip of overthinking and reclaim your mental peace.

The journey to overcoming overthinking can be challenging. It requires patience, perseverance, and a willingness to confront your fears and insecurities. But I assure you, the rewards are immeasurable. As you learn to quiet your mind, manage your emotions, and embrace the present moment, you'll discover a newfound sense of inner peace, joy, and resilience.

Remember, this book is not just about information; it's about transformation. It's about taking the knowledge you gain and applying it to your life, creating lasting change that will benefit you for years.

As you embark on this journey of self-discovery and healing, I encourage you to be kind to yourself. Progress may not always be linear. There will be setbacks and challenges along the way. But don't give up. Every small step you take towards a calmer mind is a victory worth celebrating.

I believe in you and know you have the strength and courage to overcome overthinking. This book is my gift to you, a testament to my belief in your potential for growth and happiness.

Your Voice Matters: Sharing Your Experience

If this book has resonated with you and helped you in any way, I would be deeply honored if you would share your experience with others. Your words have the power to inspire and empower others who are struggling with overthinking.

One of the most impactful ways to share your experience is by leaving a review on Amazon. *Your honest feedback helps* *other readers discover this book and provides me with valuable insights into how I can continue to improve and support those seeking help.*

By sharing your thoughts and experiences, you become part of a community of individuals committed to overcoming overthinking and living more fulfilling lives. Your voice matters, and your story has the potential to make a real difference in the lives of others.

A Final Word of Gratitude

Before I conclude, I want to express my deepest gratitude for your trust and for choosing to embark on this journey with me. Thank you for reading **"Beyond Overthinking."** I hope this book has provided you with the tools, inspiration, and support you need to break free from overthinking and embrace a life of peace, joy, and purpose.

Remember, you are not alone. You are capable, you are worthy, and you are enough.

With heartfelt wishes for your continued success and well-being,

Brianna Brooks